Poet - Linc
poetry slam

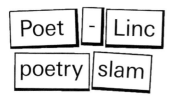

A FAST-PACED **POETRY**

SLAM FEATURING **TEENS**

FROM NYC'S FIVE BOROUGHS

PERFORMING ORIGINAL POETRY

AT **LINCOLN CENTER** TO

THE THEME **I HAVE A VOICE**

Lincoln Center

black dog
publishing

ROLL CALL

What follows is a complete list of poets and participants from the series. Not all elected to have their work published, but all of them performed for, mentored, or otherwise participated in the live series.

Bronx | Global Writes
Maria Fico (Co-President), John Ellrodt (Co-President), Brandon Banuchi, Carmelo Breton, Ciaries Martinez*, Lewis Nixon, Kaylia Rodriguez*

Brooklyn | El Puente/Urban Word NYC
Latoya Hall (Program Director, El Puente), Mikal Amin Lee (Program Director, Urban Word NYC), Nicosie Christophe, Onika Davidson, Khadjiah Johnson* (2nd place), Mikel Aki'lah Jones, Esmil Ortega, Anthony Ragler* (1st place), Angel Van Buckley

Manhattan | Girls Write Now
Anusha Mehar (Program Coordinator), Mariah Teresa Aviles, Christina Butan*, Priscilla Guo* (3rd place), Joanne Lin, Bre'Ann Newsome, Tema Regist, Najaya Royal

Queens | SAYA! (South Asian Youth Action)
Assad Naqvi (Academic Director), Saad Abbasi*, Mahe Dewan Zarif Hasan, Minhazul Hoque, Imran Khan*, Sudipta Sarkar, Mohsin Uddin, Shabab Waleed

Staten Island | Curtis High School
Tom Hepworth (Parent Coordinator), Sarah Daghestani*, Kosim Delvalle,
Darcelle Hainsworth*, Tarlee Sonie, Yusuf-Muhammed Yusuf

Emcee
Darian Dauchan

DJ/Stage Manager
Jenna Hoff

Judges
Shanelle Gabriel, Brian Lewis, Erik Maldonado, Cecilia Rubino,
audience members

Sacrificial Poets
Dorald Bastian, Lamont Bridges, JoAnne DeLuna, Nanya-Akuki Goodrich,
Assad Naqvi, Amanda Skeete

* denotes competition finalist

Declarative

Narrative

Poet - Linc
poetry slam

Free Verse

Poet - Linc
poetry slam

PREFACE

For nearly 40 years, I have enjoyed a career working on behalf of the people of New York. It remains my mission to improve our quality of life, and create a more equitable city for all New Yorkers. In the pursuit of these goals, I have been fortunate to serve for the past 12 years as Council Member for District 6, which includes the Upper West Side, Northern Clinton, and also one of the city's greatest cultural agoras, Lincoln Center for the Performing Arts.

As much as at any time in its history, the young people of New York are creating the future of our city. Their passions and transformative ideas are driving no less than a revolution in the city's economic and cultural future. As always, it is our responsibility to foster and empower them as they remake New York in their own image. To do so in the arts, they require access to literacy tools, opportunities to witness and participate in creative endeavor, and a safe—and constitutionally protected— setting for free expression.

Through my long and close partnership with Lincoln Center, I have helped to build one such environment. Among the most exciting products of that partnership is the Poet-Linc series. Over a five week period in 2012, this new interactive series provided teens from around the city a chance to work hand- in-hand with professional poets, judges, and performance crews in presenting "poetry slams". The theme for the series was "I have a voice", a title that evokes not only our debt to an earlier, ground-breaking generation of urban poets, but the inevitable rise of new voices, images, and language.

In November and December of 2012, at the David Rubenstein Atrium at Lincoln Center, I watched dozens of teens from all five boroughs take the stage in these weekly competitions. They spoke, shouted, and entranced us with images of fear, love, joy and pain, and of course hope—a great cry of honest longing, and of the courage to express in words and their music what moves the human soul.

It is often in the nature of adults to overlook the skill of the young to read the world honestly and uniquely, and to speak frankly of the truths learned there. To hear any one of these young poets create an incantation of their world— same sex relationships, broken schools, the price of celebrity, or the tragedy of abuse—was to be reminded that, like all true things formed in the crucible of life, the arts above all teach us to face what is emotionally charged, and sometimes difficult to hear or accept. This much, they insisted, is true, and it is for us, above all, to listen and to honor their word.

It is my hope that as you read this pioneering compilation of work from the wonderful young poets of New York City, you will be touched as I was, and also heartened by the vision of a world freer, and more honest and courageous than the one we gave them to begin with.

Sincerely,

Gale A Brewer
New York City Council Member, District 6, Manhattan

INTRODUCTION

This booming metropolis of New York City is filled with voices. Big, powerful voices. How does a teenager with valid thoughts, emotions, and opinions make his/her voice heard amongst the sound and fury of the city that never sleeps? It was this question that sparked Poet-Linc, a distinctive program giving area teens a platform from which to speak, to give way to their voices, to be heard loud and clear.

The Concept

Poet-Linc channels the performing arts as a gateway to promote literacy, and engage and empower youth in their community. The series connects teens to the best Slam Poetry artists in New York City while building self-confidence and their college resumes through competition and becoming published poets. Poet-Linc's first season took place in the autumn of 2012, in partnership with five community teen-focused organizations, and with the generous and enthusiastic support of distinguished New York City Council Member Gale Brewer. The series showcased the work of dozens of teens, aged 13 to 19, representing all five boroughs of New York City, from partner organizations: El Puente/Urban Word NYC (Brooklyn), Girls Write Now (Manhattan), Global Writes (Bronx), Curtis HS (Staten Island), and SAYA! (Queens).

The Competition

Poet-Linc premiered during election week on November 8, 2012, a fitting reminder of the importance of making your voice heard. For the following five weeks, the teens competed every Wednesday night at Lincoln Center. Each evening's poetry slam opened with a 'sacrificial poem' to warm up the crowd, performed by a Sacrificial Poet from the evening's partner organization. The teen poets then performed three rounds of competition:

Round 1: The Declarative Poem—a work in which the poet makes a definitive statement and expounds on that statement. It is the slam form most like a speech.

Round 2: The Narrative Poem—the poet must compose and perform a piece that tells a story, complete with beginning, middle, and end.

Round 3: Free Round—the poet may compose and recite as he/she chooses. The piece may take any form: rap, sonnet, stream of consciousness, etc.

The poets were judged by a panel of three experts and two randomly selected audience members. The highest and lowest scores were discarded and the remaining three scores combined for their round score. The two poets with the cumulative highest scores each night moved on to the finals.

The Poet-Linc Finals held on December 13, 2012, as part of Lincoln Center's celebrated free community series Target® Free Thursdays, found the teen poets performing in front of hundreds of youth and community members.

The Publication
What you are holding is the first poetry book published by Lincoln Center, and the first work from this institution featuring the words of New York City teenagers directly demonstrating the power of their voices.

This volume has been carefully crafted to mirror the live performances. Thus, there are three sections to the book, reflecting the poetry style explored in each round of competition, and each section opens with a poem from a Sacrificial Poet followed by the work of the teen competitors who chose to have their work published. Scattered throughout are additional works from the incredible mentors and professional poets who volunteered their time to nurture these young voices.

This series inspired more than just this book, these young poets gave their all on stage, displaying a remarkable level of maturity and courage well beyond their years. We at Lincoln Center hope this is just the beginning of a bold new connection with New York City's youth, and we look forward to accomplishments on the horizon for these fearless teens.

We hope these printed words inspire you to think, to learn and to know your opinions matter.

Be well, Be heard, You have a Voice.

Hillary McAndrew Plate and Jordana Phokompe
Creators and Producers, Poet-Linc, Lincoln Center

Declarative

CURTAIN CALL
Shanelle Gabriel

Is this a show
A role you play
Cause don't you know
The dramas off the stage
You light up the night
Place flames to lips
It's not a mic
In your fingertips
Yet it amplifies
Beauty that dies
With every puff
Your curtain call from life
The crowd will one day leave
This act they've seen
The smoke will clear
And you won't hear
Applause or ovations
Keep with this part you play
All that'll be left is a stage

You've always been one for dramatics
30 years playing the role of an addict
Nicotine flossing
Newport perfume
Thinking its cute but playing the part of a smoker will kill you
Think your charisma will keep you alive
While death agents are looking to sign you
Take this act on a hell of a tour
He's trying to cast you for your funeral
Theres nothing I fear more
Than watching your breath choke you
One step closer to your name in a star on heaven's door
Puffing your life away
And I'm your biggest fan
Don't know if the pain in my chest

Is from watching you kill yourself
Or from inhaling secondhand
I just want to be around you
But how can I compete?
No matter how much I monologue
The call back goes to nicotine
Follow Marilyn, Dorothy, Billie, and Whitney's lead
Allow a drug to steal the spotlight of the diva you used to be
You don't want shade from this light
It burns even through filter
You'll blame your fading career on everything else
But your own character
Perfected technique
You pull the part off so stellar like Adler
So ready to inhale this script
So doctors can hand you scripts for chemo
Protagonist and Antagonist
Trying to save the body you're killing
Everyone wants to step in
But you set the blocking
Lungs drowning in tar
Just keep swimming
And you'll be lost like Nemo
May as well write your fans a Dear John letter
Lung cancer turns legends into ordinary people
You're no superhero
Not sure if you're worth being saved
Cause you're just another addict addicted to the stage
The final act is coming soon
Drawing closer to the final page...

Mom, I spent my life with an understudy already
I can't lose you again
Step off the stage
This ain't a battle you can stay in and win
Step off the stage
Please step off the stage
No time to wait
Please strike this show before its too late.

DECLARATIVE

DEFINITION OF STRENGTH–INSPIRED BY GABE
Anthony Ragler

There are three layers of beauty:
Scars, bruises, and then the cover up
Domestic Violence is the leading cause of injury to women—
More than car accidents, muggings and rapes combined
I've seen black eyes replace mascara kits
Make believe that maybe it's Maybelline
That these violent violet bruises were her doing
And maybe he'd love her more if she was easy—
Breezy and beautiful
Girl,
You can only Covergirl so many of your problems away
When a man uses her face as a canvas for artistic expression
She embodies hues that Crayola hasn't even named yet
Cries of anguish,
A pitch that only dolphins can hear
Audio Books in Morris code
We are deaf to her screams.
Her body is a collage of sign language
Pictures worth a thousand words
She's an anthology of broken Picassos
Each slap makes her cheeks the definition of Roseart.
Eyes are swollen magic 8 balls
You can read a fortune in her tears
Each blink is a novel in braille
She's used to her spouse being more sparring partner than life partner
Wearing Everlast doesn't make the infatuation eternal
Wedding bells only remind her that there are more rounds to endure
Anniversaries sound like leather hitting broken skin
She's used to being bent, and worn out, and cracked open
How do you tell a bleeding woman that red still looks sexy on her?
That her love
Is a silent movie.
That when she's mute of desires, her body speaks volumes
And that she's as transparent as film negatives
How do you make each word a fluttering angel?

With a compliment for a halo
A harp that orchestrates revival
And tell her she is beautiful?
No Sephora products or filters needed
She is Isis in her rawest sense
Assata Shakur and Nefertiti in the flesh
Allow no man to taint her sanctity
Hands should only embrace you in purity
Abuse is not sign language
Rather acceptance of weakness.
My grandfather always said,
"Violence is a man's way of expression when he lacks the vocabulary."
A coping mechanism for futility
A failure to understand a woman's value
Beauty is only skin deep
But abuse is affliction of the soul.
The power of healing lies within those who don't realize their own strength
It is in the hands of our men,
To learn the science of nurturing from our women
For our women,
To see that they are the very molecules strength is created from
That strength is more mental than physical
Estrogen is mightier than the sword
With an ability to re-write history
With just an eye liner pencil
And that our women, are more than the centerfolds we make of them
Rather, they are the essence of everything we worship.

DECLARATIVE

17 HUES OF DARKNESS
Khadjiah Johnson

The fourth grade always felt like waking up into another nightmare
It's funny how you camouflage into the corner you walk into
My tears are probably the reason why there are large bodies of water....
I was never comfortable about my skin....
They used to say... some stupid-ish like A YO... BLACKY COCO BLITZ
I would never have a proper come back...
So I told them their hearts were darker than my favorite black leather jacket.
Their 4 chambers caged inbetween the buttons
Insults exploded and stained inside deep pockets like heated uncapped pens
I still hear the screeches from laughter of the guys who made fun of me.
I was apparently too dark for their liking....
In the 5th grade some mulatto chick always sat next to me
So whenever the boys look our way she was on the right end of the value scale
Like light skin has always been the right skin.
They compared my epidermis to the darkness of number 2 pencils
Like when they marked up scantrons
I'd be the last choice they shaded in to be with,
And they'd be out of their cotton picking mind
If they chose someone whose skin reminded them of slavery days.
They starting noticing me in the 9th grade though
When my curves developed more
AND IT SEEMED WHITE AND SPANISH GIRLS WERE NO LONGER THE CUDDLING TYPE
THEY RAN OUT OF STYLE
SEEMS LIKE BEING BLACK WAS THE NEW BLACK RIGHT?
My mother told me dark was beautiful...
But she was caramel
People compared me to charcoal...
They only use me for energy on freight trains
I'd be damn if they pressured my black tears into singing "shine bright like
a diamond"
There were nights, I had to pour rubbing alcohol on cotton balls
And try to wipe away the shame I was forced to live with called my skin.
Over the years... when I entered 10th grade sometimes I thought that
Maybe my curves were only made for people to be distracted from my face
I mean... guys always said... I was too dark for them....

Ain't nobody likes coming to the dark side....
Stuck up girls used to say "Nobody loves a darkie."
They never compared me to a brownie...
My skin was never sweet enough for them...
Grandma always said darker the berry the sweeter the juice...
Took me years to understand the true meaning behind it
Looks like my husband will be happy... I'll... make sure... he is...
That's if I'll ever be blessed to have one....
But... love has no color right?
Love... it makes you color blind...
They always said
I DON'T WANT A GIRL THAT I CAN'T SEE AFTER SUNSET....
All they can see are the white in my eyes...
Said they'll love me better if I was a white chick....
There were days I scrolled down on Facebook and saw friends who
I thought loved my beauty unconditionally
Said for some miraculous reason I ended up pretty...
For a dark skin girl.
I wonder, if every single time I admitted my feelings towards a man,
If they had to think what type of chocolate taste better....
If 99.9% cocoa would never be too bitter for him.
If their tongue will crave every inch of me....
If our relationship wouldn't be bitter sweet if my heart melted into their nerve
endings....
If they had to think would it be better to get a Spanish girl....
If I can put my hands in her hair and know there will be no tracks....
I'm a dreamer...
That has finally found the lightness of being...
"THE BLESSED" skin...
Ebony toned women always shine brighter in your eyes...
Like fireflies.
But I've once been inside of the prayer...
Being pitied for
Like I had THE BLACK PLAGUE...
Love from me... can kill someone....
I've been featured on 1000 ways to die...
Ha.
1000 ways to tear apart a dark skin woman.

DECLARATIVE

LAYERED

Priscilla Guo

I am layered
like an onion.
Like my momma put too many jackets on me this winter because she's my momma.
I am layered
Like the epidermis, papillary, reticular layers, and the subcutaneous tissue,
that make up my skin
And most people can't get past that
the layers they can see.
But the other parts
they're still part of me.
You want to take one part, two parts,
But take me as a whole.
You've got to listen, listen real close
to hear for my soul.
When you see me,
you pidgeonhole.
You put me in one role.
Ethnicity: Asian.
Slick black hair and a name
that rhymes with Ping
Really good at math,
can make some Peking wing?
When you hear me,
don't hear Asian.
I am layered
And that means I'm intricate.
Don't read that like I'm delicate
Gender: Yes, female.
And I've heard it all.
But I'm your equal
so, don't call me doll.
When you hear me,
don't hear Woman.
I'm layered
And that means I am an enigma.

Take me as I am
Not how you perceive me.
Age: 16
And that don't mean a thing.
I can be wise, immature,
But my voice
that's what endures.
When you hear me,
don't hear teenager.
I'm layered
And that means I am immeasurable even by years.
Don't dissect me
like one of your experiments in high school.
Here's the right ventricle.
There's the hypothalamus.
Here's where you listen and here's where you stop.
That's not how my voice works.
And when you hear me,
I want you to hear my voice.
Better yet, listen to my voice.
Drink up my voice.
Live my voice.
That can flow like sweet honey or
sting with bitter rinds.
I am layered.
Peel back the layers and peel back.
you'll find my voice
just like it was hiding in the back of your closet
or underneath your chair.
It dances along forever between these parts,
because I am layered.

DECLARATIVE

SHE

Christina Butan

she is my native tongue
i speak her fluently as if
she has been anchored
in the depths of my throat
she rings through my mouth
bounces off the insides of
my cheeks and unknowingly hits
the corners of my lips
like church bells chiming at noon

she makes me feel impregnated
with plants that curl and twist in my womb
a greenhouse in full bloom
she grips me like an infant
grabbing their mother's finger
for the first time
flesh hot, pink and swollen with life

i want to wrap myself around her letters
crawl into her definition where
he does not belong
do not shove him through my
blossom colored field the apples
i grow are none like the one that
sits proudly in his neck
my forbidden fruit is meant for eve
for her
for *she*
who smells like damp earth after rain
and roses left to dry

i am the querent and *she*
is the future mapped in between
my palm lines
drawn into my coffee grounds
and written in the stars
a constellation that leads
into the veins that pump
in the pulp of my heart where
i can feel her carving gently
she she writes
every curve of the word becoming
more familiar to me

(DOING ME)
Lewis Nixon

It's the young Lil Lew,
my rhyme is so dope
you have no clue,
I'll give you something very new
guess who,
(who)
Lil Lew baby!

going to school doing what I have to do to get my good education.
Because I'm an ever loving,
thinking feeling peaceful
going real life person.

This is Lil Lew showing what I do
I'm telling you bout life
and I'm gunna tell you the truth
kids stay in school
that's how you get through in life
I'm telling you this so you better let it say in your mind,
I'm a new kid trying to make a good impression,
you try to step to me
I'm gunna teach you a lesson.
Don't play rap dynasty
we the best
I'll tell you this
cuz I confess
I'm a new kid in the business
ya heard?
I'm trying to be known in the big world because I'm the mac word.
I'm gunna do what I have to do
to let all my dreams come true.
Because I'm a person, you a person
but you know I don't be cursing.
I'm the real person in the world
yah heard so listen to my words
and very slow I'm off this yo..

I AM A STATISTIC
Bre'Ann Newsome

If children have the ability to ignore all odds and percentages, then maybe we can all learn from them. When you think about it, what other choice is there but to hope? Lance Armstrong

They say I am a product of The Bronx
A product of black and I am nothing more than a location, a blip on a map

I am a statistic
But I am loud
I am a statistic and I am proud

The things they say that make me bad
Are what got me here
I have people in my corner that pie graphs said weren't supposed to be there

I am the majority
Us statistics together. A banded minority.

I'm a number and I'm a big one
A teacher's job is to help the numbers miss one

A grave stone only lists one
And a mother is there to kiss one
And I'm up here giving you the opportunity to count one
And this is what it feels like to be one
Missed kissed unlisted

I am it
I breathe it
Everyday I wake up and I see it
I walk and I live it
Forget the papers because THIS IS IT
Numbers can only say so much

DECLARATIVE

This is my voice
I am not laying on my back
Because I've made my choice

I am a statistic

I'm a number on podium a mic in her hand
So if you all could just... please try to understand

Because you all... don't know anything

You only know of what they've told you
You don't know what a beautiful lullaby it could be for police sirens to hold you
Lull you to sleep
The men cursing outside
They don't have much money
But they're having a good time
And I am sleeping tonight
But I can still hear the couple next door fighting
They're numbers too
So am I
And so are the rest you

We are all numbers

I am a statistic and I couldn't ask for very much more
Because they don't know anything
I'm aware of my number
Do you even know yours?
I understand my odds
And there's a lot of things counting against me
Yeah I am a statistic but I am paper free

And every day I'm amounting to something that statistics said I couldn't be

UNITY
Zarif Hasan

How can you see what I see?
Is it not so that our eyes are different?
Are the clouds you see the same as the clouds I see?

How can you hear what I hear?
Is it not so that our ears are different?
Are the words you hear, the same as the words I hear?

How can you feel what I feel?
Is not so that our hearts are different?
Are the emotions you feel, the same emotions I feel?

How can you even begin to understand what I understand?
Is it not so that our minds are different?
Did you see, hear, smell, taste, or feel the same things as I?

How do you know what I know?
How do you feel what I feel?
How do you hear what I hear?
How do you see what I see?

How is it even possible to know you? When I don't even know myself?
How do you even know me? When it appears that you don't know yourself?

Did I forget?
Or do I refuse to acknowledge?
Are we not all human?

THANK YOU
Kaylia Rodriguez

You raised me to have respect but
I never respect you
I hated that you are always busy
and send me to my Room
But, of matter of time, you always there for me
You were the one who supported me, not Him
but I love him more than you
I say, I hate you cause you were
Always mean and cruel until I saw
I wasn't being good
I always promise you
Ima do better but I always break
That promise
I really never meant to hurt your feelings
It's all my fault
I put you through this pain
I'm the main reason
Why you struggle
I put you to worry
coming home late
Getting in trouble in school
Sorry for what I've done
Why haven't you sent me away?
Say I'm stupid
I take that to the heart
Cause you're the one I tried to impress
But you were always there for me. I'm always angry
Cause I want your attention
You struggle to make sure
I had food on my plate
Clothes on my back
A home above me head

I wasn't making it better
By my actions I know
I'm a rotten child I know
I'm sorry
There's a few things I want to say
before it's too late
I love you more than him
he's not worth my time
I'm done
Waiting
I promise to be better
I would support you when you need it
I would make you a proud mom
You've got other child who's a success in life
You would be excited to say "my little girl is perfect"
you're my best friend
Even though you don't have time
I know some way you be there I love
You
you accept me for who I am
no one wanted me but you
all I wanted to say was
THANK YOU

BEAUTY

Joanne Lin

Beauty is defined by the
number of times he
traces your body.
It is the scent he leaves:
the alcohol meant to replace
the absence of love.
Beauty is the number of
times you can kiss without
loving.
Beauty is dark bedrooms
and empty lips breathing
full promises.
We define beauty as clothes
slipping off because he
likes you better naked.
Beauty is no longer the
independent woman but rather
the flower that opens to
any bee.
It is no longer a full heart
no longer a light touch
it is what destroys the innocence
that fails to speak in a
silent room.

UNTITLED
Nicosie Christophe

Raw from all my dreaming
I woke up half-past dead
I don't want you to see
How much it hurt
And even after months
It still does

You wanna know how that felt?
Try peeling a banana with a fully loaded rifle
Like stuffing a stab wound with razor blades

This triangle cried wolf in sheep's clothing but of course
No one believed until the wolf came

I lost two of my favorite people that day
Now all new relationships feel like digging into
a cave of carcasses
And it has an olive green odor
Its like you have to hold hands with a skeleton
Between yourself and the other person
I thought I was over it
I am not

These are not issues you flush
Hopscotch over
Or mind-bend obsolete
Betrayal is an issue you burn
Until it blackens to ashes
Until it grays into ashes of ashes
Then you stuff it at the back of your throat
Until you gag
Until you gag
Until you bring up all that you were not supposed
to swallow
Tears become your only option

DECLARATIVE

I'm guilty
Carrying around a censored plaque
Over my heart like a prison #
The glassy aftermath of my
sanity's combustion around
it like a cell wall

Well it's my jailbreak today
And I'll run through fucking glass
and hot coals if I have to
I'm not going down like that
Come at me another way
I've seen you snake before
I've seen you snake before
I've seen you snake before
I was waiting for you to shed some skin

I've seen you slither and glisten
Beguile him
Wrapped yourself around him
and took him away
I saw it all before my eyes
like I was on Animal Planet or something
And I watched
appalled yet fascinated
That day I was a lioness starved
Welcome to Discovery Channel
You know what happens to
snakes when you kill 'em?
They change color
They bend over backless into a
spring of muscles
Perhaps tie themselves like a
carnival balloon
Before the next blow snatches their soul

I'm not sure I forgave you
I said it a lot
But what's forgiveness if
the past haunts you in neon colors
And leaves you restless
Literally

UNTITLED
Darcelle Hainsworth

Giving up is like Latin
its dead
let us not revive it to the demon that it was
so it won't "Carpe our Diem"
last time it snuffed out that flicker of hope
and buried it in the dust.
Lately, its been so simple
to be intimidated and
so easy to be frustrated
but that's what fear does...
it devours commitment
hope and willpower
leaving you in a shower of razor blades,
grenades and suicidal tendencies.

it's too easy to quit
to spit out that flame of courage
as you stepped out of the womb
screaming the battle cry of our ancestors
"WE ARE HERE"
we are proof of breeding for over
a long time ago
isn't it time we acted like it?

Lets kill giving up
like how the Giants killed the Saints last Sunday!
lets show quitting who's marching out
Let us thrive on the drug that is success
and nourish our once crushed spirits
let us have faith things will get better

Lets give time a chance.

POPS
Shabab Waleed

Pop I just don't like your way
yet you hit me and throw me in the bay
and when you bring mom in this, I just wanna move away
You talk about the past
And tell me I'm always last
Like puppy who cant keep up with his mother
And yet I don't give a bother
When grades came in
I felt like it's a sin
You look at it and gave me a face
While I look at my shoe lace
Scared to think
I couldn't even blink
Then you said
You're not dead
I looked at him and asked why
He tells me I don't wanna lie
He said your my son and I'm proud
And he screamed that out loud.
I stood up and gave a glare
And thought he actually care
He said I love you son
I said I love you too
And from that day
I had nothing to say
Just kept in mind to not keep a bad moment with a parent
Cause who knows, It could be your last time talking with them.

TELLING THE TRUTH
Brandon Banuchi

Hey did you know that when you tell
the truth about something you always
get something and that's awesome
don't you think?

When I told the truth about breaking
some items in my teacher's room
and got pushed out the door
just for telling the truth,
I said to myself, *well, that sucks*
and then that's same day
I told my friend that I took his dollar
and you know what he said, *ok*
thanks for telling me!
Then I got punched in my face
and get a cool black eye.
Then I went home
and my mom said
what happened to you?

I told the truth all day and
look what it got me

thank you mother
for never telling me
not to lie it happened
all because of you telling me
not to lie
and its all your fault.

NOT-SO-REAL REALITY
Sarah Daghestani

All of these over-tanned, over-paid morons
Are corrupting the ideas of our youth
What part of drunken girls
Dressed in too tight, too short dresses
Implants bigger than beach balls bursting free like caged lions
Is classified as "reality television"?
Passed out on the floor
Wondering who they messed around with the night before
What wonderful role models indeed

Taking endless shots of liquor
Snorting god-knows-what off of god-knows-who
Nicknames all related to their six packs or breast sizes
Since when is shaking your fist and jumping
Considered "dancing"?
They all look like they got into a fight with a bag of Nacho Cheese Doritos
You guessed it:
The Doritos won

Don't even get me started on Teen Mom
Girls are trying to get pregnant to be on TV
They throw their lives away
To have sex with guys who just want to hump and dump
What kind of society are we living in
When young girls are opening up their legs
More often than they open up a book

Middle-aged women who claim to be Real Housewives
With too much money, too many plastic surgeries and are cattier than high school
Girls
Each claim to be innocent in a fight
Yet are really as innocent as OJ Simpson
All with fake nails, fake extensions and fake implants
They claim to be on "reality television"

DECLARATIVE

Scientists say each time you watch reality TV
Another novel commits suicide
Diving into the abyss of the classic TV stare
I'm in a tornado of trash
A maelstrom of stupidity
Dodging references to the 3 Bs:
Butts, Boobs, and Bucks
I have a rare B: A Brain

My reality is taking care of my little brother
While my mom is balancing two jobs
So we don't get evicted
The closest thing to partying at clubs is Bingo Night at the Friendship Club
I don't need MTV to tell me what's real

LEARNING TO FORGIVE
Najaya Royal

I hated you so much for so long
But somehow you finally made your way through my armor
A shield of mixed emotions
Into my dreams
Asking if I can find forgiveness between the cracks in my heart that originated
with you

The last time I saw you was seven years, seven months and a number of days ago
You held my hands and told me you were proud of me
That I'll forever be your little princess
But you left without saying goodbye

Communicating through my dreams
You told me to let my hard feelings go
Learn how to forgive
But this is my way of not wanting to admit
I really do miss you

I never wanted the perfect family
Because perfect is just a cover-up for problematic
But problematic would be a small price to pay to have you standing next to me
You told me, "If I could undo this whole mess I swear I would"
But could you?
And if you had the choice to stay
Would you?

Every time you would walk out of the door
You'd pick me up and say, "Take care of mommy"
Knowing that eventually it would just be me and mommy

One day you left and never came back
Leaving me with a gold heart that dangles around my neck
Where it still sits
Seven years, seven months and a number of days later
The only piece of you that still shines bright

Crossing my mind a thousand times
Residing in my heart
The man who called me his little princess
I'm finally learning to forgive you

IMAGINE...
Ciaries Martinez

Imagine...
A world
Where there are no crimes
No lies
Nobody feels hurt
On the inside
People uniting as one
No fights
Just love
A world where
No arguments occur
People respect eachother
There's no **misunderstanding**

Where bullying doesn't exist
Harsh remarks
Pushes
Shoves
Beat downs
Spanks and bangs against my crown
Blood dripping down the hard linoleum
Bruises going up and down my arm
Could this be life?
Is this what our existence has come to?
These questions flowing through my head
Like the tears running down my face
Escape seems so sweet
But the exists
Are so far away
Want to put a hault to this harsh punishment

DECLARATIVE

Where there's no racism
Where just because your white
Doesn't mean you can't interact with black
Everyone's the same
What?!?
One can be Asian, Latino
Or even African
Doesn't mean we're different

Where kids can walk around together
In a safe environment
Where kids don't get influenced by the surroundings
That are happening around them

Imagine...
A world where there's no judgment
Where we could wear whatever we want
Appearance don't matter
Where you can look like a bum or wear mix-match
Without people criticizing you
Where you can look however the hell you like

Imagine...
A world where you're proud to be human
Imagine...
A world where you can make one mistake and
it doesn't turn into a big thing
Imagine...
A world where every body counts
Imagine...
Imagine...
Now stop imagining and start creating

UNTITLED
Esmil Ortega

I'm tired. I want to be at rest like snow white.

But not even that is possible in this world, as you move with caution to advice the hurt zone.

Why most everyday feel like a repeat of the day before that, like if going through hell as a training determines weather you will reach the heaven gates.

Needless to say, I've gone through pain the endless night I spent in bed. Drenched with the mix feeling of disappointment and shame because relive life the next day to know I'm still doing the same thing I did yesterday.

We all go through it some worse then others, but everyone goes through it. You can turn to anyone for help because everyone takes their pain differently as if it was a mandatory due of pills we were required to take.

The saddest thing is that you would think that god could help, not knowing that god is at the edge of his seat while he lets his tears of saddest drench us because only he know the challenges and pain i'll go through in this life time.

"No" they would say, "You don't know what I go through" you're right I don't. But neither do you know what I'm facing so don't ever saying I haven't had a taste of pain in my life

If you're at a higher level of pain then I am then its you're fault for allowing it to get this serious. "I should of spoke up", you might think to yourself. "It's late for that now" whoever put lie into your head deserves to run laps around the outer ring of hell while there they run on the tongue letting it extend with every step so they could never talk again.

Yea, that's life for you a cruel world where even now people do helpful just to hear those two words "Thank You" as if god had just touched you with his glorious hands that blessed you with everything a human could ever want in life.

Shadow your voice for no-one; 'cause even in darkness there is always a source of light at your reach for you to share your personal opinion.

So lord bless these people who do thing to make themselves feel better or for those who do thing for the better glory of their life bless the poor for their life, bless the rich for their over expenses, bless the crocks for their desire of wanting more in life, bless those lose.

As I run laps backward in the torture chamber called hell to untangle my tongue so I may once again speak what is needed to say. In this I believe Amen.

PINCHES CUCARACHAS
JoAnn DeLuna

Cucarachas en la cama.
¡Cucarachas en MI cama!
Yo alquilé ese apartamento;
¡Yo alquilé esas pinches cucarachas¡

Que se duerman en mi piso,
Que hay mucho espacio aquí con migo.

¿Ah, que no aguantas el calor?
¿Pues sabes una cosa?
¡Hasta eso me costó!

Esta es mi casa.
Estas son mis reglas:

Aquí se duerme en el piso.
Aquí se duerme con calor.
Aquí se duermen cucarachas,
De todos tamaños, de todo horror.

Por el piso, por el techo,
Sobre brazos, sobre piernas.
Correteando bocarriba,
Correteando bocabajo.
En paredes, en ventanas,
Por adentro, y por a fuera.

Por todo el suelo y sobre mí,
¡Que no dejan ni dormir!

Si no te gusta,
¡Pues te largas!
Que yo me quedo aquí,
En el piso,
Y sudando,
Con cucarachas,
Caminando sobre mí.

¿Pero sabes una cosa?
No me importa si lo vez,
Que un día,
Yo lo hare.
—Y si no,
En que sea lo intente.

Y esas pinches cucarachas van a saber,
Que empecé de lo más bajo,
Pero llegue, hasta lo más alto.

FUCKING COCKROACHES
JoAnn DeLuna

Cockroaches in the bed.
Cockroaches in MY bed!
I rented that apartment;
I rented those fucking cockroaches!

Let them sleep here on my floor,
As there's plenty of room here,
On the floor with me.

Oh, what is that you say?
That you can't stand the heat?
Well you know what?
I even paid for that excruciating heat!

This is my house.
These are my rules:

Here, one sleeps on the floor.
Here, one sleeps in agonizing heat.
Here, sleep cockroaches,
Of all sizes
And of every repulsion.

Crawling on the floor and on the roof,
Over arms and over legs.
Running about belly-side up,
And belly-side down.
On walls and on windows,
Inside and out.

All over the floor and over me,
That they don't even let me sleep!

If you don't like it,
Well—then leave!
But I'm staying right here,
On the floor,
And sweating beads,
With cockroaches
Crawling all over me.

But you know what?
I don't care if you witness it or not,
That one day,
I'll make it.
And if not,
At least I attempted.

And those fucking cockroaches will see,
That I started from the lowest of the low,
But I reached the highest of the highs.

BEAUTY

Tarlee Sonie

Beauty is a temptress
She lures you in with lust
She paints perfection and craves away all imperfection
Beauty is an infinite concept
Beauty does not have a definition
Because it is subjective
Beauty is nothing more than an optical illusion of the mind
Beauty is just a word
A six letter word used to describe the outer shell of a person
Beauty does not dig deeper
Beauty is narrow like the world
Beauty is both artificial and superficial
Beauty is a rare commodity in this shallow world
Beauty is not in the eye of the beholder
But in the mind of the owner
Some people are beautiful
Not in their looks
Nor what they say
Not who they are
Beauty does not measure the love one has
Beauty isn't concrete
Beauty is ambiguous
Beauty tells girls to give up
No one feels beautiful because no one understand beauty
If girls wore internal makeup
Than beauty wouldn't matter
Lip glossed with ambition
Eyes showed with aspiration
Foundation of self-esteem
But all this is unlikely
In this society
All because of the narrow minded interpretation of beauty

"ACROSS THE LINES"

Dorald Bastian
c. November, 2012

Sirens
Somebody's crying—squa-le!
Another's on a soapbox saying...
X that, brothers sick of dying
And babies be crying
While helicopters are flying
Over the ghetto!
It's like Soweto!
You can ruuuuuuun, but you can't hide
From the all-seeing-eye in the sky!
It's in the elevator!
On the corner!
In the schools, on the bus spying on your mother
Your sister, your brother
And you!
The ghetto is some stuff in America!

Hey Mitt!
When you say the president bought votes
By promising new hope,
You expose your own corrupted, privileged way of thinking
Is that your politic speaking?
Or your holy conviction
that salvation is the destiny of just a fraction of the American population?
You crass and ugly fella
I see your dilemma:
Obama is the smarter, more thoughtful and inclusive brother
Lightening and thunder
Fire and fodder,
That burns your harsh surrender
to a new way of thinking and being
American.

Divisive, incisive bad taste in your mouth
Preaching an old gospel in the Midwest and South—
Whatcha talkin' 'bout Willis?
We've got this.
We, the people, we know our history.
We reconcile the counterintuitive blasphemy—
How we wrote the constitution, and turned a blind eye to slavery
How we denied our women full equality
How we (for century after century) invented crazy social theory
To promote white male supremacy.

You're singing an old song
Long gone
As antiquated as Negro spiritual
So long for that
Someone needs to give you a mic check—reality check—one-two
Instead of fat check to turn back the hands of time the way you wanna do
We've crossed that finished line with a constitutional lawyer
Squeaky-clean like Tom Sawyer
A humble servant
True American
Who aspired to be President
And won the popular vote.

And Donald Trump is garbage dumb

Full of hate and ignorance
A drowning man, grasping for straws in an ocean of scum
You talking 'bout a revolution?
We've built a new vision
Rooted in the constitution,
To form a more perfect union
Inclusive, not divisive
Forward not backward
Where eagles fly with the dove
And money can buy influence, but it sure can't buy you love.
And I know this is hard to understand
When your daddy was a rich man
And your IQ says you're an Orangutan—but dayum!
Go back to your gold-plated, diamond-studded, neon lights infested Jungle
We've heard your rumble
We see the shallow aspirations of your soul
And thank the good Lord we're NOT on payroll!

THE DEFINITION OF LOVE
Carmelo Breton

I am as free as a baby bird first leaving its nest
My nest is the busy streets of Manhattan
My current nest is the crime infested streets of the Bronx
My heritage is American for I am born here in America
But my mother is Puerto Rican and my father Dominican
So there is a little hint of it here and there
I live to enjoy the spoils of life
The treasures that lay unopened in a deserted island
I look upon the sky and wonder
Who would be dumb enough to not enjoy this?
The suspense
The thrill
The many events to come ahead
I will admit there are times when I find things unfair
Like when I got in trouble when one of my classmates threw paperballs at me
I live for the mainstream of joy, love, and appreciation
To be acknowledged by others
That is something to cherish
Love is a bond between two partners
A line that cannot intersect or break
It is a spark or a feeling that connect the two
A true symphony of harmony
An orchestra of feelings
An intertwined weave of positive emotions
That is my definition of love

DECLARATIVE

THE REASONS

Mariah Teresa Aviles

I write not because I'm happy or because I'm free, like Lauryn Hill once said,
But because I wasn't free until the pen was placed on the paper and it forced to me release,
Release the tension in my fist
Slowly unclenching my fingers, from the palm of my right hand to my knuckles until my fingertips are re-united with the pen.
The ink flows from my veins and pours onto my paper.
This transfusion succeeded and the two, slowly but surely, become one.
This ink keeps me living.
The day I become separated from my pen is the day I lose my identity. Without my pen, the facial features planted on my head will slowly melt from their original location. These features deteriorate, leaving me no destination. Soon, my voice box will self-destruct and I will then be called "crazy" and "abnormal" by those who witness me become extinct. Therefore, to keep me protected, the pen is my weapon I keep by my side, shielding me from the world surrounding, To protect, prevent, to stop and to start.
I write to prevent harm in ways that by reading my writing, a young teen girl will think twice of going in the kitchen late at night to grab hold of a knife and pierce it through her skin because she believes she has "no other choice". Yes, I write to those who suffer from the traumatic trials life may bring, providing hope in their time of need. Because while I suffered there was one who took the time to sacrifice her busy life and allowed me to read wisdom from a written word or text message
And so I write for these reasons...
I write to grab control of the roller coaster in your heart,
To strap you in the seat belt of belief,
To secure you with the locked door of that roller coaster.
My words keep you safe.
I write to raise awareness to the undercover writers.
I speak to you undercovers, I encourage you to fight your fear.
It's time you pick up your pen and put into gear.
It's your time to shine.
Your passions are shared with mine.
And for these reasons, I write...
I write to speak volumes within myself,

To show I believe.

Through this, I write to share my testimony in the Lord and let them know how good my God is. I am protected from the weight of the world when my shoulders are too weak to carry the burdens life comes with. I rather write than speak the words that flow through my mind because writing gives me and creativity the ability to process my thoughts and put them together perfectly, purposely I write to open my eyes big enough to realize that I am not where I want to be but not where I used to be either.

I write for you and me.

THE RISE

Yusuf-Muhammed Yusuf

The suffering, the misery,
The starvation, the desperation,
The constipated, they dare not say it,
For all those who faced shackles and chains, for those had disgraced for our race,
for those who didn't have the power to face them all, for those who couldn't
stand and be so tall well then listen to my call.

I say rise, and do not fall, put motivation and break that wall go into the pot
and cool that steam, break the economy don't come in to easy, because for
all we did, we deserve to win, we deserve to be free, we deserve to walk on
the streets, we don't deserve to be called the n-words, spic, chink, and every
damned word that these greedy men and bastards have called us.
No more, we can't take it, no more, we can't stand it.
Finally, I say to you, don't let them push you over and run in your house, let us
rise and stand in silence, for all those who died, in silence, so they fear us and
give us our free nation, the nation that is overall dominated by our population,
let us rise, thank you.

9-11

Kosim Delvalle

The day the earth stood still.
How many people did 9-11 kill,
and still we build over the buildings
that brought us down hill.
We leave the people looking for
their one tear in the ocean.
Words never spoken we are all hurting.
Standing proud doesn't mean your weak,
Let those feelings show letting your body speak.
I was always told actions speak louder then words,
so show 9-11 the respect it deserves.

DECLARATIVE

SO I KEEP RUNNING

Tema Regist

So I keep running.

Shackles on my feet,
Whip pressed against my backside,
Welts and bruises.
Images of my master stains my memory.
Painful nostalgia.
Rough soles that bear calluses that mark the path to freedom.
So I keep on running.

Cries of agony.
Voices of my children shout from beyond the outskirts of slavery.
All a mother wants to do is caress her child within her indefatigable arms.
Forced to relinquish my children to monstrosity,
So I keep on running.

Compromising my morality,
I keep on running.
Slavery is potent!
Begins to enslave our minds,
Don't let it enslave your mind,
Won't let it enslave my mind!

So I keep on running.
Don't let the blood I bleed fill you with sorrow;
Rather, motivation and determination.
So you keep on running!

I dream many dreams.
Freedom is my biggest dream.
So I'll keep on running till I see freedom.
Freedom is filled with elegant roses,
Soft winds combing through my hair.
Night won't be scary anymore,
Filled with glistening and luminous stars.

Freedom is just a dream.
I'm just dreaming.
I want freedom!
So I'll keep on running!

STARTING LINE
Onikca Davidson

What if your skin tone
Did not justify what you can do

Your sexuality being neglected
Afraid of whom you are
People protesting for equal rights
Army men mobilized with guns and shields

Beaten up, violated, looked down upon
Dealing with injustice

What would Dr King do
If he saw how we act today
Economy cast the poor out
Make the rich richer

Is there any hope for this generation?
This new beginning
Not so far from how we started
No change

Take it into our hands
The black community does not have
To be so low
We are here

Black girls tied to the word of a dog
An object to others eyes
Body to be used
Lips to be defile

Not realized for their brains
Lips to be outspoken
Eyes to observe
Hands to make gesture
I am a woman

Obama cannot make the change
It starts with us
It all starts with a change
In ourselves

Our image of the way we dress
The way we act
Does not tell what we can do
We have the potential
To succeed

Jails being built
Getting ready to encage us
Thinking we are no good
The black community is no good

We thrive to achieve
Work hard in class
Leap at every opportunity
Defy those who say we are
No good
I am not chained to this cycle
Cycle of not achieving
Perceptible by my grades
Define by my achievements

DECLARATIVE

Narrative

TEACHER / STUDENT
Darian Dauchan

"Uncle Darian how you do that thing with yo mouth"
Says my four year old niece Nandi
Three feet high and rising
I see her four times a year
She lives in the City of Angels
And I live in the City that never sleeps
The Big Apple
Which in her head is the equivalent to Dorothy's Emerald City
And now her enquiring little mind wants know how I do that thing I do
"Ah, you mean beat-boxing" I say
With a devilish grin as if possessing the secrets to the power of the dark side
"Yeah!". Her bright eyes widening now knowing the name
Of the mouth movement madness that has fed her curiosity
I told her "It's simple and you'll be pro in days
Have a seat and let us begin"
We assume our roles
I as guru, her as apprentice, and the course for Beat-Boxing 101 for beginners
Ages four and up is officially in session
I said the bass goes boof
And she went pf
I said the snare goes krch
And she went shiff
I said the high hat goes teh, teh
And she went tsss, tsss
And altogether real slow it goes:
Boof teh Krch, Boof teh Krch, Boof teh Krch
Which will later become
Boof teh Krch (Faster)
Followed by
Boof teh Krch (Intricate)
Now you try
And with all the determination she could muster
With her miniature mouth scrunched and lips puckered
She went Pf tsss shif, Pf tsss shif, Pf tsss shif
And I said "stop right there. That's... terrible

But you're on the right path
Because the key to beat-boxing
Is leaping from terrible to good to great"
So we start again together
Over, and over, and over again
And during my visit
Between imaginary role playing, dinner, and wrestling
We return to the Boof teh Krch
Like a mantra
It becomes the Darian and Nandi soundtrack
And every visit I make
We pick up where we left off
She prides herself in being my pupil
"Mommy, Uncle Darian is teaching me how to beat-box" she tells my sister.
And I pride myself in being her beat-boxing Yoda
"Much to learn young padawan. Much to learn"
And then the teacher has a brilliant idea
Record and review
We huddle together getting close to the speaker phone
So that we're audible, and ready to make audio magic
A voice memo master piece
Our giddiness gives me instant deja vu
Flashback to a nine year old me
With my best friend huddled in front of a tape recorder
The mini wheels on the tape go round and round
And we are recording in three, two, one
Direct and in full effect broadcasting
Live from South San Francisco on the second floor
Of the 3783 sound studio also known as my room
To an audience of two
Welcome to the Darian and Stefan show
Which regularly included long winded original songs
Choreographed sound effect fights,
Interviews with incoming callers
All with high pitched voices that sound the same
And of course frequent fart noises and fart jokes
Comically placed every five minutes within the program
Flashback to the present

And I'm in Darian and Nandi's world
Transmitting goofiness
Where the language is beat-boxing
And the currency is laughter
She learns to do this on her own
Record and playback
Record and playback
And my phone is now instantly her new favorite toy
When I leave for the West Coast on a plane heading home back East
I open my app to find a whopping 18 voice memos
Of the Nandi show gone solo
Most of it adorable nonsense
Some far too cute for deletion
Basking in her element
Unabashedly relishing in the sound of her own voice
Just as much as the nine year old me
Beat-box fumbling to the best of her ability
From terrible to good
Emulating her crazy uncle from New York
I forward the gems to my Mom and sister for prosperity
I continue to carry her voice in my pocket
And this feels as sentimental as any picture I will ever have of her
I listen carefully and take notes on her progress
So that the next time I see her
I can say "sharpen up that that bass line
Give that snare a little more kick"
So that when we flash forward to 2024
And she's crowned as the 4th female winner
Of the World Beat-Boxing Championships
The crowd in jovial chaos
Her elevated above the masses
Triumphantly raising her trophy to the heavens
And yelling "I did it Uncle Darian, I did it!"
I'll be the old guy in the back with a Mr Miyagi smile
Nodding and whispering to the stranger next to me
"I taught her everything she knows.
And I have the voice memos to prove it"

FLAME WITHOUT LAWYER

Anthony Ragler

At Poly Prep High School in Dyker Heights, former coach Phillip Foglietta
was accused by 12 players of sexual assault before his death in 1998. For 13
years, this case has been delayed going to trial. Today, we hear from one of
his accusers.

Coach said, This jersey fits me real nice.
He said he'd put me through hell.
And if I withstood the heat,
I could be the next Tom Brady.
He said I had a fiery potential.
That he còuld mold me.

The championship game vs Lincoln.
Nine seconds left, fourth quarter, down four.
A Hail Mary pass to the endzone.
The ball glided off my fingertips
slow danced through the sky
landed into Johnson's arms as the whistle sounded.
The crowd was a sea of roars.
My team ran onto the field.
Everyone was celebrating.
Coach hugged me tightly, and I smiled.
.... Coach always liked seeing me smile.
He told me it reminded him of a perfect spiral
Or an arc towards the heavens
I could reach for the stars—
on my knees.
That I shined brightest
when the lights were off.

That was when he first blacked out.
Locker room showers, he pressed me.
Goal line stance on the wall.
I just wanted to be a star.
He told me if I just did as he said, he'd make me one.
His rancid breath.
Melting the marrow off my spine.
He pressed his nails into my hips.

Each thrust felt like napalm.
I tried to pull away.
And I (stutters).

It was raining....
Skin toned whiskey down the lane of my chest.
Heartburn was never this literal before.
All I could hear was his voice haunting me....
"You're on fire kid. Let's see those flames now."
Driving the right lane of a highway to Hell;
I figured if I drove faster, I could outlast the burns.
Shoot for the stars in front of me.
An orchestra of honking horns and radio play.
A mantra of headlights and shattered glass.
Squeaky tires
And jammed breaks.
It was all a blur after that.
I only remember the hospital.
Looking into grey skies over Fort Greene Park.
The nurse's words—
My career's eulogy.
"15 lacerations. Paralyzed from the waist down.
You're lucky to be alive, kid. Coach wasn't so fortunate."

His car ricocheted through an intersection.
Killed on impact.
So were three others.

I was terrified.
Thought I was going to jail.
When I got back to school, I asked the counselor for help.
She called in the principal.
They told me if I didn't tell anyone, it would all blow over.
Said I should speak at his funeral.
If I tell everyone how great a man he was,
No one would suspect a thing.
I was his favorite player after all.

It's been over a decade.
Now,
Sundays only consists of useless prayer,
And watching athletes live out a dream I once had.
Even through the sounds of thousands of cheering fans,
I can still hear his words...
"You're on fire, kid" (repeated)
I just wish these flames would go out.

STRIPPER
Mariah Teresa Aviles

She ran track on the road of low self-esteem And rubbed the cream on
insecurity against the creases of every single curve of her body
As she was stripped
Stripped and ripped from every inch of pride
Forced to abide by rules that weren't His
But still she was held captive so those actions he took she couldn't dismiss
Her body wasn't a temple,
For it was just another tool that men used to build just another object
Objectifying every single bone, muscle, hair and piece of skin on her body
Her virginity became a toy, a ball in which boys juggled
As she struggled to own it, to claim it, to protect it, to save it.
Behind closed doors the true colors came out
The blues sung her a lullaby as
Blue painted the river she cried every night,
The sky she stared to, constantly asking "why,
Why me?"
Her voice continued to diminish
As she was still midway on the track field of low self esteem
And the cream of insecurities never dried away.
It seemed like it was there to stay,
Until she was washed of sin
And allowed the stipping and ripping from God and only God himself.
"Let me chisel away your hurt
And grace you were once stripped of"
God? That's not you!
Don't tell me love comes from a supernatural who ain't even visible when all I
know is that love ain't even equally divisible.
U wanna know what love is?
Love is
Constantly getting into relationships,
Always loving the hardest,
Which results in getting hit the hardest,
But never even thinking of leaving because that's the only definition of love you know.
Love is getting married to the fame, having an affair with the game
and getting caught up with all those business meetings.

I was stripped and ripped from the very own hands I was born into.
My body's become an easel,
Drawn with scars, never to be healed and you allowed this!
So how can you tell me I am 'loved' by the very own hands who have forsaken me?"
She asked, and He replied...
"But how can you expect one to mold a stone clay scripture?
A heart so big allowed the stripping and ripping from only the hands of man,
Which should've been banned a long time ago.
It's time to let Me do the stripping and ripping of mindless behavior and selfish desires.
You need to get stripped and ripped from the flesh's desires.
Naked we were born and naked we'll leave.
I'm tired of of seeing girls like this with unGodly mentalities
Listen, she was stripped and ripped for no price at all but for the same priceless fee,
I died for her to be."

(HELLO)
Lewis Nixon

When I first saw you, all I could say was omg you got my head
Turning
going insane.

I was new to the school and I wanted to talk to you
but it was so hard to let myself go
just to push into you.

You were the most beautiful girl I had ever seen
I didn't want to go so far with you
so you can stop talking to me,
and have me keep throwing apologies. But girl I want to get to know
you and it's like a fellow.

I'm trying to talk to you
and you got me saying

Hello Hello,
Hello Hello
let me get that info
I'll show you what I mean,
I could never waste your time
if I can get you on the line.
You got me saying hello hello,
hello hello,
let me get that info
I'll show you what I mean
I can never waste your time,
if I can get you on the line
you'll be mine.

Yea I don't know what you see
in those other guys
they are so bad
what you need to do
is to tell'em to change how they act, and it's so right because you're always on
my mind
and I swear I could show you how
to have a good time
and to let you go is like losing my soul.

Have you ever seen a worm in the apple make a big hole?
That apple is my heart and you are in it
I hope you will never make a big hole.

Hello Hello,
Hello Hello
let me get that info
I'll show you what I mean,
I could never waste your time
if I can get you on the line.
you'll be mine.

AND IT ALL STARTS WITH...
Khadjiah Johnson

Dear God,
How do you run away from feelings?
Went to the doctor's office yesterday
He told me I caught feelings and I went through multiple heart transplants to fix this.
No one was willing to give up their heart for me

So I had to settle for the desperation of the state farm jingle...
Like a good neeiiighbor state farm is there!
All I wanted was someone to flick their feeble tongue
To get rid of the same melancholic sting that's been lingering over my taste buds for years
That was said to be repaired by professional lovers.

I told them, do not break my heart.
They never listened.
So I was forced to taste their metallic type O blood through the bloody tears I cried.
Now each one of them is gone.
Our personalities started contradicted each other,

Our feelings were no longer mutual,
Nothing we had was ever mutual
The only mutual thing we had was friends on Facebook.
But there, is this guy.
That has touched every nerve cell that ran down my spine.
I felt thunderstorms rage within my body,

I felt rain pitter patting my thighs,
I imagined you pitter patting my insides.
And I am collapsing,
Under you,
Mentally, and you're not even here.
I consider love as my first form of weakness.

Thats when you don't know what you're getting into,
Because you can't fall in love.
Who FALLS in love?
The laws of love and gravity aren't the same.
You can't trip into the depths of another woman,

You can't look deep into someone's eyes.
You are only looking at your reflection through their pupils.
You can't feel them give you life with every kiss, because you were breathing before you met them.
And im pretty sure you can't get CPR with a tongue going down ya throat.
And fairytales,
They don't exist.
Snow White, what she knows about love?
SHE DIES.
A random man comes and kisses a dead body...
WHO ON EARTH IS SICK ENOUGH TO KISS A DEAD BODY?

Cinderella, she dances with a prince...
Drops her shoe, then marries him.
She could've found her man at a nearby Foot Locker.
I had my heart broken more times than Cinderella has left evidence of her one night stands.
I, never had a happily ever after.

I'm pretty sure you won't be the start of it now.
I am tired of hearing your name and feeling my heart is free falling to the bottom of my stomach.
I DO NOT CARE, IF YOU CALL AND TELL ME HOW YOUR GREATEST DESIRE IS TO BE WITH—
... So I see you decided to call.

No, you timed it.
I don't care.
I was just talking about how you make my heartbeat sculpt out of my chest.
The way you spark up my insides when you touch my hand.
The way you make my eyes gleam brighter than a lighthouse and midnight....

And the way... you...

FOCUS.

NO.

I don't care, I am not picking up that—

HEYYYY BABY... NO, NO, NO... OF COURSE I WAS THINKING 'BOUT YOU!

ALL'S FAIR IN LOVE AND WAR
Christina Butan

august
i was lonely and
i fell in like with a friend
who had strange dimples and
a forest in her eyes

september
we kissed

october
the tables suddenly
turned and there we were
face to face, ready to
ring each other's necks
with hate trembling in
her body and spite brewing
in mine her strange dimples
became strangers she had no reason
to smile at me anymore

november
a cold month with an
even colder heart nobody
knew what happened to her
nobody knew why the forest in her
eyes set aflame when she looked
at me and nobody knew how to fix
it but i knew
i knew this couldn't be fixed because
it was my fault for falling in like with
a friend i didn't really like at all i was
being punished for being selfish
for being human for wanting affection
for proving i would trade friendship
for lust

december
the trees were dead
and so was anything
that ever happened
between us

january
she fought with
her best friend and
i swooped in like a
vulture looking to seek revenge
what better way to hurt someone
who hurt you than to steal
their loved one except funny how
things work out because before i
could make my landing she
came to me instead looks like
she was also hunting for a backstab
what better way to hurt someone
who hurt you than to befriend
their enemy

february
i fell in love
not like
love
with her best friend
a complete
and total accident

march
they say things
fall apart so better things
can fall together no wonder
i never understood why it
didn't work out how was i
supposed to know there was
someone else waiting for me
and in the month where
everything bloomed
so did we

THE HUNTER
Zarif Hasan

As the hounds neared,
The fox did not fear,

Did he not know he was cornered?
Did he not know he would die?

He knew, but he stepped forward,
He knew, but did not cry,

As the proud dogs neared,
The fox did not fear,

No longer will he be hunted,
No longer they will hunt,

The dogs will be confronted,
Attacked right upfront
From this day forth,
He hunts, those that hunt,

I WAS RAISED TO...
Ciaries Martinez

I was raised to laugh and enjoy life
I was raised to walk with my shoulders
Straight up
My neck as long as a swan
And my head held high

She told me this would show people
That you feel great about yourself
That you're confident and proud
She told me
Smile
Because in life you're supposed to smile
Smile at everything
She taught me to never live your life with
A frown
Anger
Nor fear
You need to appreciate the opportunities you get...

And although sometimes she says mean and hurtful things
And I cry because I have feelings
 I wipe away the tears
And sometime she wipes them away for me
I know she doesn't mean to hurt my feelings

When I was her baby
She held me in her warm cozy arms
And said, "This is my little girl, my little princess"

Now that I'm all grown up
And I have matured
I'm turning into a young powerful lady
The woman she has taught me to be
Thanks to her
And beyond all these things

To her
I say
Thank you
My mother, mi mama, mom

SEPARATION ANXIETY
Bre'Ann Newsome

I swear as a teenager there is no possible way to hide anything
From obvious hormone-crazed fits to dealing with separation anxiety.

When mommy and daddy are too far so am I....

I remember the week my mother was admitted
I can tell you my thoughts when she first called me
"Yes, I'm free! One whole week, just me."

No cleaning dishes, no taking out the garbage can
44 degrees outside and I can still turn on the fan

But I got to tell you... in one night it got kinda lonely
No nasty dinner to turn down for ravioli
It was quiet
Real quiet
No one was yelling at me to get my uniform ready for the next day
I was all alone
Not even my little sister stayed

You'd think by the way I'm making it sound, my mother was far away

No. She was in the hospital across the street from my house.
But gosh, I gotta tell you, it's like she was on another star

That day I slept on the couch with the window closed
Because even if she wasn't there, she'd still know
That night it was quiet
And I was so alone
I'd be lying if I didn't mention that I was afraid too
Watching "Criminal Minds" in the middle of the night when you're by yourself
isn't very good for you
But I'm not afraid of the dark, I'm just afraid of whatever's in it
There was no one to tell me to turn off the TV before I went to sleep and I really
missed it

I called her and with all my mustered up sophistication...
I tried my best to say
"Mommy, you didn't call and give me a kiss or say I love you."
She was groggy and her voice was hoarse

But she still said
"Stinka I love you too."
And you guys I'm telling you that made it just that much better
And if she wanted to call me that stupid name, then I'd let her
I hung up because I new my voice would waver
So I just said "Goodnight Mommy, I'll talk to you later."

Couple of days after that I decided to sleep over at my cousin's house because
I'm a little emotional and
If I was still home alone I'd have broken down
One time, I even left my aunt and cousin laughing
And went into the bathroom and starting crying
Often we take things for granted and don't notice when we're really relying
Is it just separation anxiety or was I just home sick
My home was in the hospital and I was missing it

When she got home....

You guys there was no better feeling in the world than to whine and complain
about everything to the only person I know wouldn't throw me out because of it
It felt like the most right thing to do
Because mommy I really, really, REALLY missed you

I mean yeah, she came back yelling and fussing

And when her staples got caught in her shirt she'd start cussing
And tell me to clean my dishes, take out the garbage
And why didn't you wash this?
Pick your clothes out and what do you want to eat?
And God, Bre'ann, stop dirtying the walls with your feet!
But all of that's okay because I didn't stop doing any of those

Bre stop following me around the house!
No, because I go wherever she goes

Go to bed! Turn off the light!
Charge you phone
I love you Stinka goodnight.

Bre'Ann why are you back??
Mom, can you please just leave your door cracked!

She says gosh you're the worst
I mumble, "Well I get it from you."

"What did you say?"

"Nothing mommy, goodnight. I love you too."

9/11
Shabab Waleed

As I watch this Beautiful site
Eating my sandwich, what a delight
As I move my head up
Not trying to to say What's up
People Screaming and Bashing
While pets are dashing
Buildings in flames, no ordinary game
Glass shattering and breaking
The tower is shaking
As the clouds get darker and darker
My heart beats faster and faster
Helicopters all over the place
Business men and lawyers dropping their case
Sirens going off, People start to cough
People gasp for air , while building collapse mid-air,
Effusive ashes and debris everywhere
Knowing nothing will ever be fair

UNTITLED
Nicosie Christophe

I wasn't breathless
I didn't collapse like a punctured lung on the bathroom floor
I didn't see the blood stains
I didn't smile as I turned the key
I didn't dry my face in a hurry
I didn't bawl the few blocks home

I wasn't shaking
I leave your building a dappled leaf with caterpillar bites
I was happy and you weren't
The exhale of innocence didn't burn nor did it smell guilty
I wasn't frayed like cheap fabric
I didn't volunteer to be a victim

Somewhere in Brooklyn, in NY, in the world
There's a girl who
Doesn't know what she's doing
A girl being convinced that her backbone
Ain't sufficient to support herself
That she has an extra rib for nothing
That her feet will snap if she stands
So she better keep kneeling
There's a girl who is being psychologically abused

By a boy she barely knows
By a boy that already found her weakness

Self Image

I like your lips
You got a really nice body
Thanks, I—I think I should go
It's too soon you got me standing
I didn't mean to, sorry
You can't leave
You'll leave me blue
C'mon you know you want to

Somewhere there's a girl
confused
who thinks she's trapped
who thinks she'll get her freedom after three strokes
Just three strokes baby then you can leave

Somewhere there's a girl that did what she didn't want to do because she didn't
know what she could do.
This is for that girl
You
Your friend
Your daughter
This is for me

For the day after, when I told my best friend what
happened and she
smiled
asked, "so he raped you?"
this is for the laugh she made after

Innocence smells guilty
I wasn't happy, but he was singing
I saw the bloodstains and wish it were his and tenfold
and I did some time on the bathroom floor
But I won't lose my breath because of you
If anything died that day it was
the me who took me for granted

Don't take yourself for granted

Realize that sometimes your backbone
Is in your mouth
On your tongue
In your confidence
And you'll have to tell some people off
When they tell you
"You're beautiful"
Tell 'em
"I know"

There are too many girls
With self-esteem like steam
That vaporizes quickly
How about call it self-ESTEAM
Self-tree-root-deep love
How about call it self-cactus
Because we can survive without
Being showered by a boy's false pretense.

FRESH BLUE AND TOO EARLY

Joanne Lin

Wednesday morning the air is
fresh, blue, and too early.
Sam the bus driver stops in
front of men with rich suits but
poor souls.
The bus begins its journey,
Down the block,
Turns a right,
Slides into the traffic.
They run along
Fresh and blue
Water, men in rich suits
Complain about too early.
The bus is gliding so close
To the water so close that you could feel its
Fingers trailing down the unshaven face of
Sam the bus driver.
Running on no sleep and broken
Hopes, the water calls out to him.
Seductive and endless it presses against the earth.
Two seconds
One
Two
They free fall, men with poor souls and rich suits.
Fresh, blue, and too early.

THIS IS LIFE
Kaylia Rodriguez

*The voices in the air hear them loud and clear telling me to listen whispers in my
ear nothing can compare I just want listen.*

Her soft, loving skin her
Beautiful, long, thick hair
her body
many love her laugh, her smile,
the way she talks
like no other.

Now her skin so rough and scarred all over
by the way you take that wire and
smack it across what once was a beautiful face

the way you called her names
breaking her into shredded pieces beating on her like she was worth nothing
the blood dripping down her face
tears roll down
out of her eyes
begging you to stop but you don't stop
you grow angry and angrier.

Each day you abuse her
the more you know
she grew weaker and weaker
she couldn't handle a drunken father
always beating her

One day when no one was looking she choked down pills coughing
dying slowly
she knew he wouldn't care
so she popped some more
dying the next day
on overdose.

See she once had a happy life with a mother and father. Loving and caring for her.
She was a good girl hoping for the best wishing her life was better
She used to sing to her mom every night.
She cried each night, cutting her skin, wanting to die.

She tried speaking up but no one believed her thinking
She liked
She wished
She hoped
anyone could kill her. The way he laughed in her face making her feel worthless.

Look what happened she took her own life

Her voice wasn't heard

Each night we pray at night knowing her soul is in heaven's hands.

Speak up!
Where's your voice?

UNTITLED
Esmil Ortega

Boom! The sound of a gun scares others because they don't know where the bullet might take its next vacation.

Until Snap! The lady I love it hit messing up my vacation. Running to her side dropping to my knees "please don't leave me, I ain't ready to take on the world without you" but she's far gone only God could see her.

Now this sadness becomes a twisted idea of pain and anger. Planning a torture chamber worse then any horror movie seen. But relating to all the paranormal activity movies where the predator can't be seen.
Nor heard!

Every breaking swing taken by the same item that Babe Ruth hit those amazing homeruns that lead the Yankees to their victories.

My mind becoming twisted. The eyes of this young poet just went from a glare that puts a smile on people faces, to a
pitch-black darkness that can't be related to the night sky
or a black hole.

The metaphors being used leave you gasping for as if you were drowning in the depths of the ocean because you thought a human couldn't have such a stair.

An idea that you thought only existed in movies or in cartoon shows. But hey if the lady that brought you into this world was killed you would become a one-track road, or better yet a narrow minded killer.

The bullets as if trained to be an assassin that eats, sleeps, lives, and feeds on killing like if peoples' souls contained all the vitamins needed to give you those strong bones people talk about.

A bloody scene that not even the worlds best-trained detectives couldn't find a single clue. A quick in and out. Unseen and unheard like a shadow in the night.

The young man sits down, playing with the beloved like this idea of man's best friend.

Meeting face to face with an angel sent by the heavens above.

The kid comes back to his senses as if the flame that had awakened the beast sings it a lullaby to put it back at rest.
The sleeping beast is fast asleep in seconds.

But the boy still left without the other half of his heart. And to
think she had two other little ones, how do I break the news to them without the water works playing a major roll?

And to think that the bullet landed at the wrong destination, mislead by the wind from the screams of the crowd that
was around.

The lady that had open her wound for the bright child to come out was gone.
Taken by the wind in a second. Unseen. Unheard!

MARCH 4TH, 1992
Eric Maldonado

Last night I was an eleven-year-old too consumed
with his video games
to spend time with his bedridden grandmother.
The old soul whose conservative ways
kept me in line but whose liberal love
fed my spirit.
I've always wondered
what I would've said
or done, if I knew
you weren't going to wake up the next morning.

I play out in my head
that I would share one last dream with you,
I'd explain how the boogie man
and the monsters in my closet
left me alone because they knew
you were protecting me
and how the doorway to your house
filtered out my insecurities.

We both know,
I probably would have just cried.
You were the first piece of my heart I had to bury.

I'd like to believe you can hear me.
I wish you the power of x-ray vision
so you can see how my DNA strands
twist and turn
the way your cursive writing did.
I'm just waiting for a sign,
a text message or voicemail
letting me know that
you knew how much I appreciated
everything you did.

NARRATIVE

I need you to know that oxygen doesn't smell the same
and the colors of the world have faded out
in the my wash of tears.
Memories of you have yet to dry
though I tumble through them like a dryer.
My smile is in foreclosure,
I can never pay you back.

4 March, 1992 feels like everyday to me.
The day you passed away
and someone hit
the reset button
on my life.

"ADDICTED POETRY"
Darcelle Hainsworth

I wanna fly can you take me far away?
give me a sign to reach for
tell me what it takes
and I'll get so high, I'll get so high
my feet won't touch the ground
this is my crutch
I need it much to rock these dreams
or I'll fall down

Let 'em come,
the heavy metal rattle
the eff off face
her own personal battle
she draws
graffiti stains her hands
a cool cat
street cat
nobodies fan

let 'em come
the morphine, the heroin
she'll never feel better and
the poison fills her veins
she lets 'em get the best of her and
she dresses like a he
so she wont have to bleed
nobody will see
her body
she's a closet woman
cut hair and all
shes so afraid of the climb
so afraid of the fall

her art was mostly comics
she grew up reading as a tot
Batman, Superman
DC comics and pot.
her favorite canvas
an abandoned parking lot
turned into a garden
full of broke cars and weeds
she'd visit at three
always on time.
that's when her 'inspiration'
and gone went her mind
when she wasn't high,
or painting up the street
she was in a nursing home
always on her feet
being told war stories, 'bout the 50's
the age of swing and jive
the age of rebellion
off these stories she'd thrive

let 'em come
forget the cops
forever on the run
she was Lost.
never found
both her parents
underground
her artwork world renowned
she's a rebel
inhaling toxins as she drew
so afraid if people knew
she was a female they would
take away her spray paint
the only source of her joy
and leave her with kids
as if it were her role
she got inked on her eyelids

let 'em come
the ambulance
an overdose
overdone
on tippy toed perscription pain killers
killing the ache within
she was bleeding
from within
her stomach eating
her organs pinned
the light
fleeting
she whispered
"my name is Bruce Wayne , and I kill people"
she blanked
in her hand, a half empty bottle of spray paint

her last felony cried "WE DON'T EVEN LIVE HERE!"
surprised authorities when they came to get her lifeless body

THIS WORLD
Brandon Banuchi

This world is destroying every emotion I had inside
and I don't think I can get them back from the bad things
I have done.

I try and try
to fight every day
and the people
I care about have also been destroyed with my emotions.
But all I see now
is darkness everywhere
and can't hardly breathe
this world is never going to change.

I feel paralyzed and can't move
and every emotion
is drained out of me.

I fall into a complete fade o dust
but I try even harder than before
To stand to my feet
and say to myself
I will not be beat
and take what once was mine!

STRONGER
Tarlee Sonie

All her life she was deemed different
She could never fit in
She was an outcast
They teased her with words laced with venom
Ugly, Ugly, Ugly
So she changed
She did her hair a new way
She wore different clothes
They made fun of her
Because her clothes were cheap
And her hair was nappy
They made her feel unwanted
When all she wanted was acceptance
She wouldn't take no for an answer
So she did the only thing she could do
She changed
She tried harder this time
Did new things
Spoke differently
Gained new interest
They laughed at her
At her pathetic attempt to fit in
They called her darkness
They made fun of her accent
They distorted her image of herself
Now all she sees when she looks in the mirror
Is what they want her to see
She once had a voice as loud as lion
But they tamed her voice
Till there was nothing left
They pulled on her strings
And moved her left and right
She didn't say anything
She became dead inside
Soulless

Living life without a purpose
They took everything away from her
Her creativity, her originality everything
After years of being a puppet
She finally cut the strings
Now she imprisoned in her mind
Her over analyzing mind
She became an introvert
She stuck with her thoughts
Her only friends are the ones her minds ponders up
She enjoys the solitude of her mind
No one judges her their
No one points finger their
No one laughs their
She feels like everyone hates her and the world is against her
Low self-esteem
And social anxiety
Hide behind her 1000 watt smile
Would you be surprised if I said?
That girls was me

MS SOUL
Najaya Royal

It all started when
Hip-Hop found its way from her lips to my ears
Educating me on something real
She opened my eyes with her rhymes
And ever since I've been
Awake

Ms Soul sat with me
Holding my adolescent hands within hers
She told me I had a gift
Learning to let words flow as they please
Forming a story that can warm the coldest heart

I promised her I'd never abandon my gift
And I'll never forget what she said
She told me for the first time in months her tears were finally filled of joy
I was her newly born Hip-Hop

Years passed by
Our lives went on
Her existence started to fade like the ending of a song
She began to slip through my fingers
But my memory held her tight

It would be a while till I saw her again
Probably years
She was standing in a public restroom
Disheveled and unaware of my presence
It took me a while to recognize who she was
Because her body was now a prison to her soul
A prison she can't escape
She washed her face with rough paper towels
Focusing on her reflection in the mirror
She again spoke of Hip-Hop
Her first and only love

She was not the same Ms Soul that held my hands tight
She was long gone
Trying to free herself in a public bathroom mirror
I wanted to help her
She finally broke away from her gaze in the mirror and looked me in the eyes
I turned away and ran out that bathroom
Not wanting to remember her that way
So all I can do is pray
For Ms Soul without her namesake

UNTITLED

Mikel Aki'lah Jones

In first grade I was the most
talkative kid in the class
I was the little girl with ideas
coming out of her like fireworks
I was a boss
I thought I could change
the world with my voice
My teachers would smile and say
something like
"awesome" or "ok"
But no one ever said I could do it
As time went on teachers saw
less and less in me
My voice became a whisper in the back of the class
The class clown in fifth grade
I put my voice in my locker
Speaking became harder for me I
became the most invisible
And the most quiet
My life became phone calls home
long walks with the guidance counselor and
people asking me 50 times a day "Mikel are you okay?"
I held my thoughts in for so long
when I tried to speak the words
never came out right
Every time I tried I just sounded weird
I I couldn't even write a poem
to express how I feel
I went from invisible to the awkward one in six months
I tried to be proud of my awkwardness
but my tongue wouldn't let me
I tried to be confident
But my spine wouldn't let me
I ran home every night to scream
I cried for every low participation grade

and unsuccessful conversation
I hate my fear
I hate my brain
I hate silence
I wish I wasn't a slave
to what people may think of me
I prayed that I could be as confident
as my father's laugh
Why can't I just raise my hand and speak?
In seventh grade people started to hear me
and I thought it was beautiful
I'm starting to think I am beautiful
I hope you wanna hear me too
And now, I'm actually at a point in my life
where I might just actually
be something beautiful

DEAR FATHER
Sarah Daghestani

Age seven, you were gone
It was as simple as that to my young, scared eyes
Gone, and not coming back
Why, mommy?
Why isn't daddy here, mommy?
And before she could respond

Memories of the past seven years come flooding back
Memories... of hiding in the closet, hoping you wouldn't find me
Memories.... of you beating me with the metal pole
Memories... of you calling me a liar, and beating me refuselessly

And for what?
Going bowling with my girl scouts troops
Memories... of times when my head used to lay on your lap
Now... washed away with the images of my head in my hands
Countless sleepless nights
Wondering where I went wrong
And why you're still gone

So much for being daddy's girl
When you live in such a cold and abusive world
Though the scars on my pale skin have faded
The wounds on my heart have not
So much for being daddy's girl
When you live in such a cold and abusive world

TAKE ME AS I AM
Onikca Davidson

Makin' holes through the wall because you don't understand
When you're gone you don't see how I am treated
You don't hear what they say
Coming home drunk and unable to walk right
Her body has so many handprints in them that she hides her skin under those long sleeves
During the day she can't look at her kids as a mother should
Her body was so many times defiled
Her lips still had the drunken bitter taste
All she can do is put her own two hands in front her face to hide herself from reality
But those fragile hands can't cover up those open wounds
Your tears can't wash away the endless night lying in bed with a stranger
Your memory can't be void with fantasy
Dreams no longer have significance to you
Only survival matters to you
Waking up again to just slip into your tight dress and walk out that house to repeat it again

Truth or False
People want to experience love when it's not even there
There it goes again
That smile and that tone that puts you to ease
That touch that draws you in closer just before your conscience says wait
You don't want to talk, you don't want to share your feelings, you only got one thing on your mind
Using "I Love You" as your tool to draw suckers in closer
You're telling her sweet play on words just so she can lay still for you to have your chance
Using your hands as a conversation to her body
You don't know what she is feeling deep within her
How her emotions ply into every corner of her mind
Her parents see that you're no good for her
They realize the game your trying to lure her in with
Not a shame of how you're tearing her apart easily
When you touch her face, can you see that smile she makes is not genuine?

When she's alone she cries....
She cries because her insides are like a dirty alley with busted glasses
Drenched with that after smell of erosion
That smile that once use to show sunshine is pitch black....
Are you satisfied now?
Sick and tired of seeing that smile you use on everyone
That touch that once use to send her heart thumping now leaves

END OF THE EARTH PLACE KNOWN AS THE WORLD

Yusuf-Muhammed Yusuf

The door opens, into a gastric explosion of the universe, a universe never seen before, as the knob separate's from the lock, the eyes of a young soul enters the confusion state, as the life of this young boy is revealed.
(The boy speaks)

Where am I? What happened? It looks like I'm not even supposed to be here. I feel so out of sight, is this even real? I see a big explosion, and I see the other planets, where is the Earth? Why am I able to breathe in space? Where is the rest of my human race? What happened?

As the boy figures out what is going on, the constant certainty of the world is unknown. This as it was foretold was the end of the world, it happened earlier than expected. The young man survives out of 250 trillion humans in the world. It's impossible to believe, but as the life of this boy unravels there is more than just a speech.

Somewhere in the far distance beyond the Milky Way Galaxy. A ship in the sight between granite and calcite as the fusion of cold and heat interacts with his ship, the captain that is appears as an invisible object passing through space.

(The captain Speaks to the Colonel)

Colonel we have seen a living organism, in the far point beyond, should we save the soul?

No, we have no time to waste as the destruction of the universe is at stake

But what if this organism happens to be the one, you know
the one who can save us all, as you can see he is the only
thing that survived from a huge explosion of a planet
is that not strange to you?

You may be right.

Suddenly, everything fades and the young boy realizes everything that he had envisioned was a dream, and he is uncertain if that dream could be a vision, the life of this young boy is unknown and unforetold, if he knows, how long would it take for him to realize that he is just a puppet in the universe of the gods.

WHO AM I?

Tema Regist

Who am I?
A dreamer who has an imagination that is its own world.
A seeker who will go to the ends of the earth to find what she's looking for.
A creator who loves to create works of art in poetic formation.
An optimist who believes there is something so magical about the world and
how it impacts humanity.
Ms Independent,
Glaring eyes of ambition,
Soul full of success.

Mommy always told me to reach for the stars,
Yet when I reached,
I landed on the moon,
As I dance to the rhythm in which poetic words roll off the tongue of my mother.

See, peer pressure was always a flaw of mine,
The urge of wanting to be with the in-crowd.
Cuz see, being smart wasn't always easy.
Empty brains and the aroma of marijuana seemed to surround me.
But mommy ain't raise no fool.

Feeling like the lover who has never been loved,
Piercing hearts of despair,
Loving someone who neglects the fact that you exist.
So you ask yourself "What is love?"
How can you believe in something that you've never felt?
See…
Because when I fall…
I fall hard.
But no one is ever there to catch me.

So I allow my dreams and nightmares to take me on adventures.
I'm too young to be feeling this kind of pain.
But, young no longer has a definition so....
I listen to love songs and have Cinderella on replay,
Waiting for my glass slipper to be found.

Instead tears run down my cheekbones
—Not as a sign of weakness,
But as a sign of strength.
See, memories don't go away that easy.
But...
Time goes on,
Life goes on,
And your heart breaks again.

MALALA, MALALA
Priscilla Guo

Click, the sound of the indifferent gun cocking back.
That's the last thing she heard before they shot her.
But that's not the last thing the world heard from her.
We forget and travel in a herd
So the lines that separate get blurred
We let them just take the last word
And it's a little absurd, and a little backward,
That we should be censored, Shot.
But excuse me, sir:
Malala Yousufzai was 15.

Before, she said:
We scream through and through
and through. Not enough desert sand
can be stuffed down our throats to keep the words from flowing.
We band together to fight in sisterhood.
We have no money but we are richer than most.
We have the words that affect the mind that thunder through the hills, that
shakes the roots of institutions
the words that change the world.
"I think of it often and imagine the scene clearly. Even if they come to kill me, I will
tell them what they are trying to do is wrong, that education is our basic right."

The Taliban hissed:
"Yousafzai is the symbol of infidels and obscenity."
Treacherous words. Serpentis.
Encasing her, encircling her.

They hunted her down,
like she was an animal, subhuman.
They had her surrounded and
they stopped her yellow schoolbus.
And the masked gunman shouted "Which one of you is Malala?"

Where identity means death, instead of
that first day of school where you shyly say I am Malala.
Where you tremble to say your name for fear they were listening for it.
Where things are better protected behind closed doors.
Malala was silent.
He hissed again: "Speak up, otherwise I will shoot you all."
And he would
just so he could stop the one girl.
The fifteen year old girl who had power against Goliath.

When they shot her,
they forgot that words stick,
to the paper they were written on; to the ears that were listening;
words stick and voices are heard for centuries.
I am Malala.
The girls chant from all around the world
I am Malala
because her voice lived on
I am Malala
and she lived on.
I am Malala.

Free Verse

YOWL
(A HOWL FOR MY STUDENTS)
Lamont Bridges

I saw the young minds of this website generation pinballing across tangled
    infected internets, skidding vacant bored
joysticking themselves through the hallways of routine, weaving winding past
    a blur of bodies, fast forward, with faded map and crippled compass
anxiously poised to leap from childhood's conveyor belt, wearing disposable faces
    seeking some sort of sense and sanity and security
who hangout brokenmouthed on streetcorners and in livingrooms, keeping
their distance
    channel surfing with remotely detached controls steering their virtual sitcom lives
who master the art of juggling the hours and days, competing with clocks whose
    arthritic hands refuse to cooperate
who stride streetsmart and beautiful, flirting with virgin daybreaks, trying to buy
    six-packs of confidence from junkfood bodegas rooted in vacuum-locked
two-by-four neighborhood grids
who shoot holes in their education, rolling bullets and blunts from the torn-out
pages of classic novels,
    coldstaring down grandfather's wisdom, amputated from their once sweet
leafy souls
who ache for the harvest, fertile soiled, unseeded, thirsty, laughing in the
sunlight of
    innocence, dancing to the electric heartbeats of elastic youth
who stand undaunted on the edge of the cliffs of adulthood
    inflating with the urge to fly
who ride the song of a brave new flower, daring an old world to follow,
    flying with the urge to love.

JUNIOR SEAU'S FAREWELL
Anthony Ragler

"I never made a deal with the Devil,
But I broke promises to The Lord
I tried to be the man I should,
But sometimes I fall short
I'm not a man of anger,
I never meant to hurt no one
But there are things in my life
I'm sad to say I've done
Cuz I broke the hearts of angels
Cursed my fellow man
Turned from the Bible
With a bottle in my hand
My only hope for forgiveness
When the good Lord calls my name
Is that he knows who I am....
And who I ain't."

Somewhere along these lines
I lost my sense of self
15,000 concussions over a 12 year span
Can do that to a man
My name is Junior Seau
And football is the only identity I've ever known
Once upon a time
I made my family's name synonymous
With greatness
Nowadays their faces have been casted into a shadow of my memories

I met my son again today
His name was
He asked me if the NFL was worth losing my sanity
If the fans screaming my name was the only reason I remembered who I was
Or if I loved his mother as much as my play book would I still be home

FREE VERSE

I responded by asking him for his name

I'm not too good with short-term retention these days
I can't tell you where I slept last night,
Or what her name was
But she knew who I was
And I could tell her the stories of how I was once a gladiator
Who made quarterbacks fold like prayers
I traded in my Sunday Best for a helmet 19 years ago
Still, fans would praise my name like His
I felt holy here
As if my Hall of Fame resume could bring me closer to Father
Or crucifying my body on the field made me more like the Son

But the afterlife of retired NFL players is far from heavenly

78 per cent of NFL players will be alcohol or drug addicted, divorced, or
bankrupt within two years of retirement
I was all three
The NFL is a world where you're judged solely on your statistics
So I've always gone above and beyond,
Even if it meant my downfall

The legacy outlives the body
I wanted everyone to remember me
As immortal
Reason why I never showcased my pain
Never was diagnosed for concussions
I knew I had
Played through injuries

Persona of an Alpha male
All the while a struggling soul
Abyss to a mirror
All vodka and Ambien
Enhancers to misplaced anger

The person I am would bring the person I should be to tears
I'm not in control of this corpse of a vessel
My mind isn't mine anymore

The legacy outlives the body
But the mind is puppet master
What is a legacy if you can't live and remember it happened?

The rate of suicide for retired NFL players is six times the national average
For many of us, we've died long before we take away our lives
When we put our helmets and pads down for good
Life loses its purpose
But when my mind tells me to forget my purpose ever existed
I become an empty casing of the man I thought I was

When you find this farewell,
It will already be too late
I just ask you to fulfill my last request:
Donate my brain to the NFL's study
Make sure no one ever has to suffer what I have

When the spotlights finally fade
And the #55 jerseys are retired for good
I pray my legacy as a man
Isn't tarnished by the remnants of the superstar

THE R WORD

Christina Butan

don't say the R word
because when you do there is a
a rush in my stomach and my palms begin
to sweat and i feel anxiety creep up
on me like an unwanted visit from
an old friend.

don't say the R word
because that is why my lover sits alone
going crazy in her own home
gasping for air because her nightmare
will never be understood.

don't say the R word
because i'll find a way to use it
as a reason for why everything falls apart
i'll transform it from
the beautiful thing it is meant to be into
the tormented soul of every believer
i see.

don't say the R word
because books were written to tell
stories not to craft your life around them i mean
if that were the case i would be getting
on my knees repeating little red
riding hood's pleas, looking at the three
little pigs as my saints and claiming i
could speak to the little mermaid.

don't say the R word
because saturday night everything is
fine with her hands in mine but
come sunday morning they quickly press
into prayer; her family thinks
she's committed a crime and so does
the big man in the sky who
is allowed to have a say in this because
it isn't enough that politicians tell me
who it's okay to love but a guy with no trace of
existence also gets his own judgment call.

don't say the R word
because you don't need it
to have morals, good and bad can't
be taught, we feel what's right and what's
wrong in our gut, don't stand there and
tell me that my kind of love is wrong
because at least i can base it off something real
while your reasoning against it
doesn't have much going for you at all.

don't say RELIGION
because it's not death we should be
afraid of but how we will die and
it's not looking too well for the human race
if we continue to preach, this disease
will only grow and soon enough
it'll wipe out everyone you know but
before we rot in our graves i can only
hope that my last words go a little
something like this:
i told you so
i told you so

FREESTYLE

Lewis Nixon

School got me bored
taking tests all day
it's making me snore
and that's not great.

You hear it from me
not only my crew
I rap so tight
man, this is what I do.

so I can't wait to get out of the school
I can go home and do what I always do.
I'ma gonna stay on the top and stay for a while
I'm not gunna drop the ball so I can get that crown.
Wooo solo.

Spitting these tracks with a brand new rap,
my name Lil Lew but yah all know that.
My flow so hard,
my flow so nice everybody like my style because it is so dang nice.
Lewy everything, Gucci everything
everybody tried to come at me because I'm doing my own thing,
it's all right because I'm gunna be on the top and when I do make it
people going to be like *what?*

I'm so bad
I'm a bad boy when it comes to rapping my style's so unbelievable.
Yes I'm back
I got mad lives,
I'm untouchable you can't see me
word life.

DISASSEMBLING THE HEART
Khadjiah Johnson

You used to have a home here, now I have no idea where you went.
It's gonna take me more than the few years I spend adoring you to vent,
All of the feelings and pain been pumping into my veins for 1,461 days.
They say love hurts but in the future it pays.

So I wanna ask you a serious question...
How many fantasies does it take to take to get to the center of a teenage girl's heart?
Seems like entering a closet to get to Narnia makes more sense than till death do us part.
About 151 million pulses I thought pulsated in-sync when it was really offbeat.

I tried to pour my love into your left atrium but the process wouldn't complete.
I pounded his chest asking him to let me through the four chambers of his soul.
Our world is "scientifically impossible" so my blood vessels are forced to pay the toll.
This is what I get, going for the good ol' Christian boy right?

Now it's like when I'm fed up I'm standing in pure darkness without a skylight.
Damn, now I'm holding this knife craving to be the cause of his death.
I don't know if I want him to gaze me in the eyes before I take away his final breath
Watch my passion pass through his aorta now, ahh love kills.

I was willing to give him all of the compassion, wonders and the thrills.
Well God is at the glorious table conversing with the angels during heaven's final meeting.
Im wondering is it a sin if I clutch the left ventricle before it contracts so his heart stops beating.
Shhh need to drop the knife thou shall not kill,

Well I can say his heart skipped a beat when he saw me, and his body just laid still.
AH who am I kidding? Gonna be written up in the book of evil, I don't need this now.
Well, I can always go to Russia, settle down in Moscow.
But they say you can't run away from God so I got a bit of a problem there.

Slight issue guy of my dreams, his heart, his brain they're having an affair.
So, if I block his superior vena cava I won't be the one in fault correct?
Apparently not, there is more than just surface problems I'm forced to dissect.
Dissection of memories, but I'll collapse to the ground in tears if I have to go into detail.

Amazing how I inhaled perfection, but its painful when corruption is all I exhale.
Maybe heartbreak is what flows through my veins instead of blood.
My heart stuck in a drought in the middle of an emerging flood.
I beat my heart dry.

I bet he thinks im gonna cry.
Cry over what?

Over him, again?
Well there are other men, I used to think he was a perfect ten... divided by two.
My vision of love wasn't a heart plus me subtract you.

Guess mathematical equations doesn't work in complicated situations like this.
Well now im the x that never happened and y was compassion and it square rooted us.
Haters need to realize them living is less than or equal me running them over with a bus.
So if love became the only religion available I would probably become atheist in the long run.
Im done with everything MY HEART IS PHYSICALLY DONE.

Love starts from heart, and the feelings flow through your body like blood circulation.

Till this day I'm on my knees, praying to God I won't be the start of the new heartless generation.

WHITE FROST

Joanne Lin

The streets are empty and the snow is white.
He exhales smoke from his lungs.
She inhales the breath from his lips.
They stumble through the dark.
He runs his fingers through her limbs.
Her body trembles on the bed.
The night is tangled in her sheets.
He takes her off his chest and leaves in the morning.
She pulls the scent of his body into her.
They wander alone in empty streets.
The snow is white beneath their toes.

"MARIE ANTOINETTE"
Darcelle Hainsworth

I am a queen
sitting pretty in my castle
getting what I want, when I want
piece of cake.
Peasants pretend pawndom upon me
so I jumped them
all the way to my crown
MY CROWN
this is MY town
and this is where it all went down.

Guards guarding a self-proclaimed goddess
never trusting
always watching opponents
Jumping cities with my rooks and knights
there is no king in sight.

I AM THE QUEEN
commanding bows when I speak
when you walk into my palace
you better wash and dry your feet
and beg mercy or I'll have you arrested for treason
...
or for no reason.

I am the queen

FREE   VERSE

or so I thought
my once pure heart of gold had started to rot
and I began to walk like the lifeless
but what surprised me the most

was the taking of my crown
the seizing of my city
the riot in my town.

my once loyal guards now seized me

my once loyal subjects now humiliated and stoned me

they took my crown and crowned a new queen

and as that final stone hit me
I realized, I'm not a queen
but a servant,
to desires that tempt me.

THE INEVITABLE
Zarif Hasan

In the silence of my company,
I heard without my ears,
Saw without my eyes,
The endlessness,
And at the same time,
The nothingness.

In the company of my friends,
I heard with my ears,
Saw with my eyes,
My endlessness,
And my nothingness,
Together in Harmony.

I live now,
Carrying on the company of myself,
One day the inevitable will come,
All that will remain,
Is the company of the world.

THE AMBITION TO EXHALE
Bre'Ann Newsome

> *Character cannot be developed in ease and quiet. Only through experience of trial and suffering can the soul be strengthened, ambition inspired and success achieved.* Helen Keller

I may not have that much money or expensive clothes in my closet
I may not have many electronics or extensive dollar signs in my pocket
But what I do have is ambition and a handful of courage
And I'm willing to do what ever it takes until it works

My mother doesn't own a car or a Prada purse
And it may be raining on top of my last name
But I've seen worse
And I've been called worse
And expected to achieve lower
But I refuse to stop running until this race is over

All of the other kids may have jewelry and their jeans identified by the brand
But I have a quarter in my pocket,
Two pennies in my left hand
They all may doubt me
And nor does anyone see
The greatness that has been endowed and is so deeply rooted within me

I am greatness
I am phenomenal
I am the tallest mountain
Amongst these brown-bricked buildings you can see

I can write
I can speak
And I am the best... by far, at being me

My dad doesn't live with me
And nor does my brother
Yeah she's flawed
But you've got me mistaken if you think I'd want another

They may have seen me trip
Slip and stumble
Tear, blink twice
Curse, heard me mumble
But I promise you they will never see me break down or fall

I have a point to prove
To myself, competition, their mothers and all

I may not ever be rich
But I don't mind being well off in a condo
Don't need to own a company
But a small business fine, make it mine pronto

I have the longest history of never going too far
If you look into my background you can get the hint of why I'm trying so hard
So hard just to find an open ear
I have the kind of luck that if I knock on someone's door,
All of a sudden no one's there

But I don't care if I get turned down
I will find someone else who will listen
Because they will hear me and all that I have to say
Hear my voice, my way
Rain, snow, hail, I don't care

I will fight and thump and knock down doors until I find someone there
Whether you all like it or not I will prevail
And when you see, you ALL see

I will scream, cry, smile
And then Exhale

MY HEART KNOWS THINGS
(THINGS I WISH HE KNEW)

Kaylia Rodriguez

My heart know things, things I wish he knew
my heart
the muscular, multi-chambered organ
my heart
damaged and drained since he left,
my heart
that pumps, receiving from the veins
there by maintaining
the flow of blood,
my heart
going through hell
without
a father's love
hoping for the truth
only receiving the lies
My heart
knows things
things I wish he knew.

I wish he knew
I still have hope of him being my father.
When everyone says, "Let him go, he's useless!"
I say "No".
I wish he knew
I miss those good times
when I was little
he would try
and scare me in dark and say, "I'm coming to get you!"

I wish he knew
I still miss him.
When he used to ask how much I love him.
Or the times he would get me what ever I wanted.
Daddy's little girl.
But now I wish
he knew.
He loved vodka
more then me.

Knowing that he'd rather
spend his holidays with another family
That he'd rip my heart out and
Not give a damn no more.
The day
he laid his rough hands on my mom,
soft beautiful skin
the day
I lost respect.

I wish he knew
each day my hatred grows more and more for him.

He would always come back saying "Kaylia, come on, were going out Friday."
Every time
the day comes
excuses after excuses
he was just with his little girlfriend
My heart
is torn apart
like pieces of paper, shredded.

FREE VERSE

I wish he knew
I want my father back.
The one that always has my back.
The one I can bond with; I can be myself with.
The one who makes fun of my toes.
The one I called ugly.
The one I look like,
not the one who drinks,
can't even keep a job.
Not the one who picks his girlfriend
over his little girl.

My heart knows things,
things I wish he knew.

DEAR SOCIETY
Sarah Daghestani

Dear society, desensitize me
Lecture me with more of your rules, society
The world is your aphrodisiac
So you stay turned on every minute
Giving off new vibes, new rules, new trends
They set the standard of what is 'acceptable'
Your cruel, judging eyes
They're watching me
Every second I breathe
You use greed as a weapon
You kill me with your continuous rules I must abide by
Got me checkin' out those,
And checkin' out these
I'm not exactly sure just what you want from me
Mainstream me, disinfect my breed.
I'm looking for nirvana, a greater perhaps
But you decide to over-polish me
Anoint me with your lies until I am the 'perfect' me
The me that you want me to be
If heaven is the goal, well then point me the way
I won't lie my way in, no faking IDs
I'll die standing, fighting for the right to be me
Try and break me down, get me by the knees
I promise to never bow down to you
Don't act like you know me because you recognize me
You sell my record, not me
I am the music man
And you sell the music
Not the soul that creates it
Not the heart that FEELS the lyrics
You sell my record, not me

FREE VERSE

I WOULD DIE FOR YOU
Brandon Banuchi

I will die for you
you're my life
you're the person that always comes into my mind.

I have so many feelings for you
that it doesn't even slip my mind everyday thinking about you
makes me glad to be with you.

When you're happy
I'm happy. That smile always brings out the sun.
I have never felt this way ever in my life,
ever since I laid eyes on you.

You're my life and soul
you're my light to get to heaven.

My only way to get to heaven.
I want to die old with you that's number one on my list.

That will never change
no matter what.
If you die I will kill myself,
just for you and me to be together

You're my everything
Can't live one day without seeing you.

If I don't
I won't
know what to do
and why can't you
understand that I will die for you.

UNTITLED
Shabab Waleed

I hate that you're you
You used to be my boo
But now your just too much
It feels like I'm stuck in a bunch
The lies that broke the trust of us
Looks like you wiped it off like dust
Doubts poured in to the broken crack
Making more pressure and hurting my back
Hate is all I gain from this
Makes me wanna throw up that we even kissed
Change is something that never ever came
But you just took everything like a silly game
Mistakes that happens you kept on repeating
It felt like all I got was a good beating
This love and this hate is burning me away
But you just kept walking and I had nothing to say
It's true we used to be like lemon and lime
But now you're just a waste of time.

FREE VERSE

PARADISE

Tarlee Sonie

Do you ever just sit and ponder?
Do you ever let your heart just wonder?
Is it incredible out there?
In your own little world
No judging eyes
No passerbys
This must be what heaven feels like?
You're delusional
Open your eyes
Are you disgusted by the filth of this world?
The cruel and inhumane behavior
There is no savior in this world
Just bestial human beings
Who would trade their soul for a hundred grand
This is paradise
Don't blinks or you might miss it
Horrific killers with words as their weapon
This isn't human nature
Mindless people who worship animosity
This is paradise
The world is cold
People plaster smile on their faces to hide their sadistic grins
Ignorant minds and irrational behavior
Leave the world entrance in chaotic fear
This is paradise
The world is full of mindless chatter
People shying away from open minded thoughts
Doors locked, curtains drawn
What wrong?
This is paradise
Secrets we try to hide will aide in our demise
Building blocks of animosity cause worldwide genocide
A prayer unspoken
A wish one dares not utter
This is Paradise

MACHIAVELLI
Carmelo Breton

I justify the means
Because I know just what you mean
When you go to flee
And by any means
You're survival is so crucial
To watch for Jabberjays
And become delusional
In a mystical realm
Is this real?
Is this hell?

Get out of that stance
And out of your trance
Because when you justify the means
I know exactly what you mean.

THIS IS HOME
Mariah Teresa Aviles

I have no control over my body
yet my body has all control over me,
Pressure grasped to pick each foot up to walk;
My upper body follows immediately after.
The train doors kindly allow me to exit its territory
And as I do it the favor,
I enter the station,
The platform,
A new whole world;
This is my kinda world.
"This is East 125th Street."
Almost every hand raises,
And so my eyebrows raise in confusion as to why.
African hands bang against the faded white African goatskin on top of the
brown, carved, hourglass-shaped wood.
I'm home.
Sound waves flow from her vocal chords out of her mouth and into the air.
They meet my ears,
But go through one and out the other...
And meet at my lips.
And as I tap, tap my hands on my lap
And stomp, stomp my five-and-a-half size kicks on the ground,
My thoughts gives my words a voice,
Speaking through the music surrounding every inch of body,
Providing rhythm and style.
I am the lyrics to a slow jam,
Accompanied by spoken word,
My words are learned from my audience,
Being encouraged to spit some more,
Spitting my lyrics into the pierced hearts as healing.
And as I make it back to East 125th Street,
Those African hands comfort me,
As they bang against the faded white African goatskin on top of the brown,
carved, hourglass-shaped wood.
I'm home.

I DON'T KNOW
Ciaries Martinez

I don't know what to write
I don't know where I should begin
I'm so bored, nothing is flowing in my head
I don't know
I don't know
I don't know
They tell me to use my imagination
I don't know
I don't know
I don't know
I feel like my head or brain isn't functioning very well
I don't know
I don't know
I don't know
You know why I don't have nothing to come up with
Maybe it's because I don't like writing poems
I don't find the meaning to it
I'll write it because I have to but
If I had a chance I wouldn't write it
Not even a line
Not even a word
I don't know
I don't know
I don't know
But I think I just wrote a poem

TIME MASTER
Carmelo Breton

When I say you can't see the past without seeing the future,
You come to the past to be a loser,
You fight again and again,
And then you lose her,
What do you now?
When there's no future,
You can't see both anymore,
Can't you tell that you've got your moral?
To go back you must know what happens forward,
Don't you see it's too much stress?
You can't save her,
You need rest,
You can't breathe.
The miasma is turning your eye red,
You can't send for her,
You can't lend a hand,
You can't think straight,
Her curly red hair,
Her glossy pink lips,
Her bright smile which reaches farther than a mile,
Now your time is up,
It's revolved around your head way too long,
Now you've stretched your reason far too long,
To go back and save her,
To go back and be braver,
Than you ever were,
Don't be as scared as you were,
Be a Time Master,
Be a valiant soldier,
Brave the woods,
Brave your conscience,
And hold her tight,
And don't lose sight,
Of all those memories,
In the back of your mind,

It makes no sense,
You're getting confused,
You need her and she needs you,
Time is the key,
For me and for you,
Time is the key,
And good luck to you,
Don't lose sight,
Don't you move,
Behind your fright,
You fight your way through

FREE VERSE

LIFE
Yusuf-Muhammed Yusuf

Life.
It is the way people live,
The way we eat, drink, sleep
And think about their thoughts from within.
Life is about survival.
The only thing keeping alive
The only thing that makes you strive, for more.
The pains in life will determine
What your future will be,
The joyous parts of life, that you will always see.
There is nothing wrong with the choices you make,
It is how you start, or how you put yourself in place.
No one has a better life than anyone,
Just because you are rich, it doesn't make you the perfect one.
Don't compare life with others,
Life may be different for one another.
But we are equal, and we should
Treat everyone like our brothers, and sisters.
Life is hard, there is no doubt but without us, what is life about?
There is a question that we all have at the end.
Is it worth living, when you don't know, where to begin?
Where to start or where to stop, where to think about the consequences,
Where to not, it's not about life, it is about us, because we make decisions of our lives,
Sometimes we think it through, other times we don't.
Does that make us fools?
We are not perfect, this is true.
Everything they do is because of you, they sacrifice their needs to nourish you,
But who told them not to think it through.
Like I said everyone in this world isn't perfect, this we can all see.
We thank our God for everything, from the parts of our body to the jobs we get.
From the benefit of being alive, till our memorable death.
What will you make of your life that you won't regret.
Life.

ON SKINS AND STORMS
Amanda Skeete

Part 1:

... foul cerebral storm-stenched senses with sagging death;
a sweet smell of strange fruits tight-roped my vocal chords,
left my tongue engorged—
the static in your hair planted suffocation and dry tornadoes inside these lungs.
My monsoon season was a whiplash of long black tresses,
a cascading darkness crashing around my heart and stealing
s(c)en(t)se from my mind.

... I can't count how many times your laughter ignited the **Charybdis** in you—
how many times I became your flotsam and jetsam—
can you blame me for *ship*-wrecking this body of mine?
Sheets—strangled limbs—lifeless in patches of moon-skin at night,
catching the Eye of a whirlpool only precursors a raging symmetry of flesh
burned off the brow,
bolstered by your mother's trident spitting lightening—

Calypso begot the beast.

... If I swam far enough from the gnash of your teeth,
it wouldn't erase the days you tried splitting my skull with your chubby fingers
and Siren-song.
I slash-reduce-**engulf**-darkness-*peace* you repeated till my sight grew numb.

... You hold life lost in your fists,
taunting me with time.

You will not win.

FREE | VERSE

Part 2

One-track see-all peerless mind,
side-winder,
sign-blinded;
forget that I'm slipping away from you with the sheep,
forget the sharp pain in the center of my forehead,
forget that you forgot to blink—
remember only the continent you threw at my escape attempts.

Africa.

Darkness of skin,
darkness of heart—
no wonder your lungs go *bump* in the night—
you breathe to the rhythm of the Congo.

Yellow-ocher clay fingers—
the malleable molds color into vanity.
i-Spy,
u-Spy,
singular dosage-drops of melanin corrupts,
the half-breed sapling bent in fetal fear by burdens too great for its age,
you only see me in shades of **blackness.**

If a Cyclops could see in pairs...
Perhaps colors would run in twos and threes the way my complexion does.

We would be grey.

UNTITLED

Esmil Ortega

Words of a Wise Poet. Well at least I consider myself someone.

They say that anything that is thought of can be made or considered a poem.

But I can't get the thought out of my head, that even a boy my age can be arrested.

The idea of society is rhetorical to me.

Government is down the drain. The mayor of New York is completely worthless. Right now the only I believe I can count on is the president. Well I hope I can.

It gets me mad to think that all races can be judged by other races because the behavior or the way a certain person would act. It's like a big stereotype. It's frustrating to think that this is how we're seen by society. It's like "does no one care or see wtf is going on around us?!?!" But I would never say something like such in person.
Some things are just best left unsaid. I feel as if I have to take action and responsibility for my race and all other races that society only sees. But hey why stress myself about all this. I'm not a super hero. And yes I have heard the saying "one person can make a difference" but what they don't know is one's voice can only be heard from so far it's impossible for my voice to raise up against humanity. But at the end of the day. It's better to know I am someone. A poet!

LOST

Kosim Delvalle

He sits alone in his room,
thinking about the lies
that lead him to this new world of lies.
Having flash backs of getting beaten
being in a tight hold and not being able to get
free asking for forgiveness for something he may cause
then he snaps. The twisted fate of a young killer a
never-found child things like this get people exiled.
Now he's compiled with too much and attacks the one
he held dear, but that was just the start of this letter
he ended lost in his mind looking and fight for a way out.

LOVE

Kosim Delvalle

A feeling many people feel love,
the key to the soul.
A broken heart is a broken soul,
so know love before it could get
a chance to know you.
Don't blind yourself by what you want,
but by what you feel.
Love equals lost of versatile emotions.

FREE VERSE

UNTITLED

Tema Regist

The sun didn't set today.
Sleepless nights for Mother Nature.
Oceans twisting and turning on their rocky sea beds,
What once was beautiful.
Pride blinding the people,
Refusing to heed warnings.

Cold water slams against the bodies of the helpless.
Ocean water neck high,
Hands spread wide open,
Grasping and clenching onto Mother Nature.
She tortures her children.

Clamoring arms that tremble in fear.
The elegance of the eye that stares down at us.
Swirls of danger,
Outraging force driving through the sea,
Tropical wonders that kill and destroy.
Fury!
Rage!
Muffled cries of despair.
Shattering windows.
Agony pushing and pulling on front doors.
Frustration relentlessly ringing doorbells.
Mother Nature in hysterics as she splits open doors.
Splinters stab the people who stand behind them.
Her wrath trails her.

"Rain, rain go away. Come again another day."

Sand grains thrust though air,
Soft gasps for air,
Nostrils with no oxygen,
Heart beats slow down in unison,

Boom boom   Boom boom....

Vibrations of dying people,
Wind that turns trees full circle,
Obliteration of roof tops.

Mother Nature on sleepless nights,
Expect the unexpected

UNTITLED
Mikel Aki'lah Jones

I've been living in this cold paranoia
jail cell for years
I'm scared of loss
Because she left
Me sitting in front of her lifeless body
She promised me she would be ok
Chemo was sucking life out of her
so when she touched me
I could see death on her fingertips
Usually a mother's love is shown
by her touch but I haven't
touched my mom in five years
When she died the sky rained
all the tears I didn't see
When I was 12
Crying had become a daily routine
I wrote poems into my wrist
The feeling of hospital beds and metal
have been embedded into my skin
I wanted to slowly fall apart just like my mother did
They called it depression
I was addicted to sharp objects and pain
And even on the sunniest days all I saw was rain
And somehow I found this beautiful
Basking in the gloomy mornings
that would break my spirit
I would embrace it
but who would be proud of a scar
that's eating them alive
And nights I wished God would give me death
because maybe when my heart stopped beating
I could feel her hand
caress my back
again

BUTTERFLY BOY
Najaya Royal

You were just a shadow in a bright room
Young and alone
Left behind to go to war with a million dragonflies
You've outgrown your cocoon
And the ones you felt the most for
Saw you but really never noticed you
So you escaped into your own world
Pretending the sides of your worn-out wool coat were wings
Wings to carry you to places only a child could dream of
Butterfly boy, you don't live in a valley of multicolored flowers
You live in a place where alleys are the darkest
And your ability to succeed in this world is highly doubted
This was once my story
Existing in a place I really didn't belong
Held down by time and burdens
Wondering when they would set me free
When I see you
I see me
More than scraped knees and salty tears
There are dreams behind your brown eyes
You are not a shadow
You are light
You are one
Yet you are no longer alone
You are not easily classified
Simply, you are different
Spread your wings and fly
You are Butterfly Boy

FREE VERSE

LISTEN

Priscilla Guo

Listen. To the song here in my heart
The melody I start but can't complete.

ego habeo vocem.
I have a voice,
in the five languages I know,
I have my voice,
out of seven billion people.
And a voice.
It's this beautiful dialogue between yourself and the world.
Where you know you're being understood in some way or another,
Where you know you're understanding yourself.

No matter what language I use.
I speak. You listen. And you understand with your heart:
She has a voice.

Because identity transcends vanity, it transcends names and places,
it transcends that effervescent humanity,
it rises higher and higher
and climbs faster than we know.
Because it is not something we know. It just is. It's just what we have.

We have always strained
for our voice to be heard in the crowd
As though hearing it aloud
would make it endowed
with an audience.

You put it out there. Hoping it will catch and attach
itself onto someone's tympanic membranes.
Someone must share your truths.
Hurl it to the stars to the depths to the heights,
to the shades and the lights.
I speak to defy limitations and change expectations.

I speak with enunciation, punctuation, and preparation
  to change.
  to echo. to last.

Ode to the voice that has left me with choices
I rejoice.
I rejoice.
  For I have a voice.

WHERE ARE PHILOSOPHERS TODAY?
Asad Naqvi

Let's begin with a quote...

> *Ghostly roads, reflecting the icy deception of a sky looking down grinning and faceless, Dear friends, beware of the thievery of clouds, hiding in plain sight, banking on our bashful downward gaze. The coloring of ambiguity, the shades of fog, brutishly painting over everything the eerie darkness, the presences of an absent sun... the philosopher is marked by this, the taste for evidence and the feeling of ambiguity.*

Where?
In trenches, gathering in groups holding hands?
Bombarded by the exploding embers of collective memory and pop
Self proclaimed honors of time spent curing the curse,
Free for all, so long as they're chosen
Revolving doors never open never close
Yet, wage on under the smutted sky, like cutters
Dirty hands, covered in ink, filled with blood,
and dancing with panic
Shivering cold over the thought of thought
A stark raving idiocy over language and action
Always crashing, overcoming a harshly addictive passion
Today, the cause seems dead and yet the weaponries remain,
Simple intensities, like a fashion who knows of no end
Diligent climbers,
Performing detail and self reliance through the garb cloaked over their shoulders
Truly colorists, crudely cut from the winds of clear and distinct ideas
Just breathing, the march on time comes to collect
While wise homely earthlings fasten tight to metals
Dwelling in sculptures of wholesome catharsis
A memory of regrets and attempts
Fools to think, all glorious moments bask in the white sunlight of intellect
Fools to think that pointed pens presses into trees flesh will cast magic into the world
Fools because they know better than they do
Trumpeting catch phrases and cultural critiques,
What if this isn't enough,

If there can be no dance to the music of canceled and rescheduled appointments
What if the shrieking Styrofoam cups, plastic faces, and empty gestures
Grow too loud to find anything in public space
There is a penalty for asking questions and a penalty for not participating
A fee for paying the fee

Replay:
Brace, remember we fixed propellers of marble and gold
The others think all poetry is just coupons for government subsidized empathy
Not free, but cheap love
Void where prohibited, see details below, disclaimer, disclaimer, disclaimer,
But the philosophers see, a fantastic seizure and spastic resolve,
"It doesn't seem like better fuel economy will stop tragedy from happening"
Where are philosophers today? On stage as sacrificial poets
Mutants, deranged and diseased, coughing up smoke signals
For those watching over the air and all its invisibilities
Speaks, "I am never going to sleep again, I am neon, strong as poison,
Eating the sharpest radiation, like words out of books,
A magic on their hearts, a monstrous howl
There is no shame in desperately summoning one's own bravado
We can turn ketchup packets into human bodies, powerful and bold
Let the colors be shown, even under threat of estrangement or obscurity.

CREDITS

Katherine Farley
Chair, Lincoln Center

Reynold Levy
President, Lincoln Center

Hillary McAndrew Plate and Jordana Phokompe
Creators and Producers, Poet-Linc, Lincoln Center

Russell Granet
Executive Director, Lincoln Center Education

Tom Dunn
Sr Director, Concert Halls Operations, Lincoln Center

Rebecca Arnold
Director, David Rubenstein Atrium, Lincoln Center

Andrew Kalish
Director, Strategy and Business Development, Lincoln Center

Godfrey Palaia
Production Manager, Lincoln Center

Brenda Cooney
Associate Producer, Poet-Linc, Lincoln Center

Kio Shijiki
Producing Intern, Lincoln Center

Production Crew:
Andrew Blais, Timothy Knapp, Dorian Mancuso, and Michael Nazario

ACKNOWLEDGEMENTS

Special Thanks and Open Mic:

We at Lincoln Center would like to take a moment to thank those folks who donated their time, effort, knowledge, and funds so generously to making Poet-Linc and the publication of this book possible.

NYC Council Member Gale A Brewer, Telepan Restaurant, Wellness in the Schools, Bill Telepan & Jimmy Nicholas, Reynold Levy, Liza Parker, Dan Rubin, Russell Granet, Peter Duffin, Betsy Vorce, Martin Schott, Celie Fitzgerald, Black Dog Publishing, Duncan McCorquodale, John Ellrodt, Maria Fico, Latoya Hall, Anusha Mehar, Mikal Amin Lee, Assad Naqvi, Tom Hepworth, Darian Dauchan, Shanelle Gabriel, Jenna Hoff, Brian Lewis, Erik Maldonado, Cecilia Rubino, Dorald Bastian, Lamont Bridges, Joanne DeLuna, Amanda Skeete, Nanya-Akuki Goodrich, Tom Dunn, Tamar Podell, Jennifer Berry, Rebecca Arnold, Andrew Kalish, Matthew Troy, Godfrey Palaia, Brenda Cooney, Kaitlyn Meade, Leaha Villarreal, Jonathan Bench, Pablo Santiago, Christena Gunther, Hannah Heller, Marian Skokan, Kate Merlino, Corina Bardoff, Kio Shijiki, Rita Ombaka, Caitlin McCarthy, all of Visitors Services at the David Rubenstein Atrium, and the parents and guardians of the talanted teen poets, for permitting them to participate in this new series.

Use your voice:

If you attended Poet-Linc or read this volume and are inspired to share your thoughts, please write us or email us at:

Poet-Linc
Lincoln Center Education
(212) 875-5535
70 Lincoln Center Plaza, 7th Floor
New York, NY 10023

PoetLinc@lincolncenter.org

COLOPHON

© 2013 Black Dog Publishing limited, Lincoln Center and the authors.
All rights reserved.

Black Dog Publishing
10A Acton Street
London
WC1X 9NG

T +44 (0)207 713 5097
F +44 (0)207 713 8682
sales@blackdogonline.com
www.blackdogonline.com

All opinions expressed within this publication are those of
the authors and Lincoln Center, and not necessarily of the publisher.

British Library Cataloguing-in-Publication Data.
A CIP record for this book is available from the British Library.

ISBN 978 1 908966 26 1

Black Dog Publishing is an environmentally responsible company. Poetry Slam
is printed on sustainably sourced paper.

Lincoln Center

art design fashion
history photography
theory and things

www.blackdogonline.com